taste of naples

taste of naples

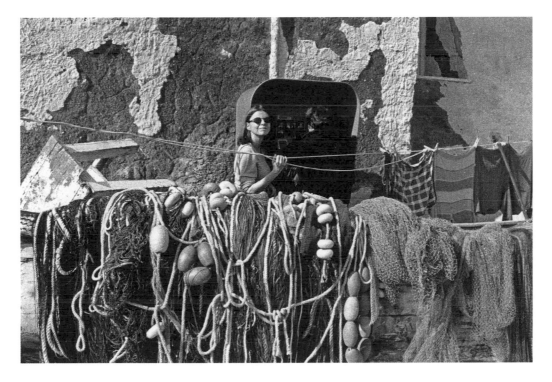

ARTURO IENGO

IN ASSOCIATION WITH I.R.V.A.T.

NAPLES PHOTOGRAPHY BY HANNAH MORNEMENT

NEW HOLLAND

CONTENTS

Introduction   6

Appetizers & soups   12
  Olive oil   20

Pasta & rice   30
  Mozzarella di bufala   44

Main courses   66
  Regional wine-making   72
  From the sea   90

Side dishes   106
  Coffee culture   110

Pizza & bread   124
  Wood-fired pizza   126

Desserts & pastries   136
  Festivals & celebrations   152

Index   158

INTRODUCTION

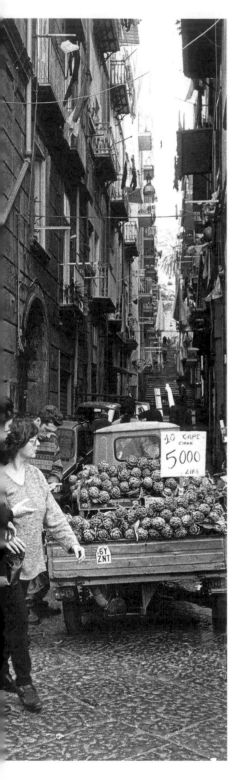

With more than 500 hundred kilometres of wonderful coastline, two national parks, a vast plain and spellbinding mountain landscapes, Campania is a rich and diverse region offering all the variety you can imagine.

The long history of this region has left a deep mark on the archaeology, on the monuments, the secular and religious architecture, on the character of its people and on the warm hospitality that always amazes first-time visitors to Campania. It's the ancient land where Ulysses and Aeneas roamed, a land of myths and enchanting mermaids. A land which has been lived in and loved by great artists, whose creative genius can be recognized in the architecture, sculptures and paintings in which the region is so rich. A land to be visited and discovered; from the traditional crafts of its artisans, to its characteristic produce, from its distinctive wines to its lively cuisine, and to the songs and music that crossed over the boundaries of the region to conquer the entire world. The ancient Greeks and Romans, the Arabs, the Spanish and the French have all left their mark on this part of the world that has so many traditions of its own to offer.

Campania needs to be enjoyed from village to village, from local tradition to local tradition, from corner to corner, to appreciate the full range of the land and all it has to offer. You can take your pick from the wonderful islands, the enchanted coastlines, the engaging vistas of mountains, rivers and lakes – every twist in the road or turning of a corner seems to offer a unique sight or a new experience to explore, all within easy reach.

The history of the region has also left an indelible mark on the cuisine. Innate appreciation of fresh produce and reverent treatment of food so that nothing is wasted are woven into the very fabric of daily and cultural life. *Cucina povera*, or poor man's food, is a prime example of this, where fresh ingredients are used in simple but flavourful combinations to make the most of what is on hand. Fresh vegetables, pasta, pulses and seafood dominate, with historically very little meat in most of the diet because it was beyond the means of many people. What meat there is tends to be pork, lamb and kid, with beef used more rarely and often being cooked for a long time because in the past the cheaper cuts were all that most people could afford. Chicken does appear in the regional cuisine, falling somewhere between the two categories. Today, the regional cuisine is still very much dominated by the precepts of *cucina povera*, with Campania's provinces, cities, towns and islands all making their own contributions with key produce and signature dishes – lemons, walnuts and dairy products from the Sorrento Peninsula; more lemons from Procida; the beloved San Marzano tomato of the Amalfi Coast; mussels, bluefish and Annurca apples from the Phlegraean Fields; rabbit from Ischia; *mozzarella di bufala* and chestnuts from Caserta; apricots and cherry tomatoes from Vesuvius; anchovies, artichokes and figs from Cilento; truffles and mushrooms from Irpinia; hazelnuts and walnuts from Benevento. The provinces of Benevento and Caserta give us their hearty peasant cuisine – as well as *torrone*, *nocino* (walnut liqueur) and Strega – while the island of Capri brings us limoncello and *insalata caprese* (see pages 112–13). In Naples, specialities include spaghetti with clams and, of course, pizza marinara and pizza Margherita. This list is by no means comprehensive, nor is the produce necessarily confined to the places named; it serves only to illustrate the wealth and variety of what is so abundantly available in Naples and its surrounding districts and islands.

The region's food is also greatly influenced by the kitchens of the convents and monasteries of the Catholic Church. Not only did these institutions often cultivate great market gardens and sell their produce, but the Church's policy of providing food and shelter also meant that many great dishes have emerged from the convent/monastery tradition. One such example is the pastry *sfogliatelle* (see pages 146–7), now a popular Neapolitan speciality and sold in bakeries and *pasticcerie* all over the city, but which was originally concocted in the Croce della Lucca monastery, where it was made for visiting prelates.

And there is yet another layer to the cuisine of Naples and Campania, one provided by the royal and noble households of the past, under the rule of the Kingdoms of Sicily and Naples, the Spanish viceroys and the later Bourbon court. The first had the effect of bringing spices into the kitchens of Naples, through alliances and trading with the Arabs (Naples was at this time a great port, with links to Genoa and the major trading routes of the time), while the Spanish were in power at a time when they and the Portuguese were bringing back new and strange fruits and vegetables from the New World – hence the arrival in the Neapolitan (and Campanian) diet of what are now staples such as tomatoes, chillies, potatoes and beans. Under the French, chefs of the Bourbon court were brought from France and made their own influence felt in the form of rich sauces and ragùs, and what has now become the quintessentially Neapolitan *babà* (see pages 150–1). The more you look at the regional cuisine, the more complexities and interweavings you discover – all bound by the people's zest for life and their open hospitality.

AN ANCIENT WINE TRADITION

Campania has more to offer than a cuisine which excels in combining tastes and adding layers of tempting flavours. The region also has a long and fascinating history of viticulture. Legend has it that God wept when he recognized the Bay of Naples as a limb of the sky torn off by Lucifer; where His celestial tears touched the ground, the so-called Lacryma Christi (Tears of Christ) grapevine sprung. Between myth and legend, viticulture in Campania dates back more than 3000 years, to the time of Etruscan settlement. The region is, in fact, scattered with archaeological remains and other evidence that testify to the long presence of grapevines and to the excellent quality of wine production. Wine was exported from Ischia during Roman times, for instance, and mention of Campanian wine is made by Horace.

Today, Campania produces on average around two million hectolitres of wine per year, of which 135,000 hectolitres are certified DOC (Denominazione di Origine Controllata) and DOCG (Denominazione di Origine Controllata e Garantita). The former certification relates to the origin and production of the wine, the latter does the same, but with an official guarantee of origin.

Specifically, there are three types of DOCG wine: Taurasi, Fiano di Avellino, and Greco di Tufo. There are, on the other hand, 17 DOC wines: Aglianico del Taburno, Asprinio d'Aversa, Campi Flegrei, Capri, Castel San Lorenzo, Cilento, Costa d'Amalfi, Falerno del Massico, Galluccio, Guardiolo, Ischia, Penisola Sorrentina, Sannio, Sant'Agata dei Goti, Solopaca, Taburno and Vesuvio. In addition, nine types of wine, both reds and whites, have a certification of regional distinctiveness (IGT, or Indicazione Geografica Tipica): Beneventano, Colli di Salerno, Dugenta, Epomeo, Irpinia, Paestum, Pompeiano, Roccamonfina, and Terre del Volturno. (For more on regional wine-making, see pages 72–3.)

Fortunately both for Campania and for wine lovers, viticulture and wine-making have undergone something of a transformation in the past few years, with standards and production techniques improving, new vineyards being planted and renewed energy and commitment being seen right across the industry.

SORRENTO CHEESES

This renewed energy is being seen across other agricultural sectors as well, lifting the economy and rejuvenating interest in products that have long been produced in the region, such as particularly fine mono-cultivar olive oils (see pages 20–1) and *mozzarella di bufala* (pages 44–5), to name just two. While *mozzarella di bufala* (buffalo mozzarella) is undoubtedly the most well known of Campania's distinctive regional cheeses, it is by no means the only variety that has its roots in this region.

The Sorrento Peninsula is an area with an ancient dairy tradition. At the beginning of the last century, Sorrento dairies supplied Naples with their products twice a week. The dairy products were placed on mallow leaves and shipped by rowboat across the Bay of Naples to the capital. That level of industriousness is still in evidence today, and towns such as Agerola on the Sorrento Peninsula are renowned for their quality cheeses, and especially for *fior di latte* (literally the 'flower of the milk' and made from cow's milk), *caciocavallo*, ricotta and *provola*. *Fior di latte* is made in the same fashion as *mozzarella di bufala*, with the same separation of curds, which are then stretched into shape by hand. The making of *fior di latte* is another of Campania's ancient traditions and has official PDO (protected designation of origin) status. The most famous *fior di latte* is produced in Agerola, a town whose origins date to pre-Roman times. During the time of the Greek physician Galen in the second century AD, Agerola was already renowned for the production of 'very healthy milk'. Top-quality cow's milk has always been used for the production of *fior di latte*. This cheese is thus an integral part of the dairy heritage of Campania. It is spherical in shape and sometimes slightly flattened, with a white colour that is less chalky than *mozzarella di bufala*, from which it can also be distinguished by its firmer texture and more delicate flavour.

Another important local cheese, *treccia sorrentina*, can in turn be distinguished from *fior di latte* by its distinctive shape and even firmer texture. Some dairies fold the extremities of the cheese, creating a shape that is reminiscent of a *tortano* (a type of Easter bread): this product is dubbed *tortaniello* locally. *Provola*, or provolone cheese, also has a spherical shape, is more or less flattened and has a firmer texture than *fior di latte*, more like *treccia*. Its outer rind is whitish or ochre in colour, which is not uniform when smoked (*provola affumicata*).

THE TOMATO – HALF STAPLE, HALF RELIGION

You cannot help but notice how many recipes from Naples and Campania involve the tomato. This fruit is so beloved in the region that people have been known to say that it is almost a religion. The *pomo amoris*, or *pomo d'oro* (literally, 'golden apple'), may be of Peruvian origin, but it speaks the Campanian dialect perfectly, thriving and prospering in the climate, and fitting seamlessly into the region's traditions and cuisine. This is particularly true of the San Marzano plum tomato, grown mainly in the Agro Nocerino-Sarnese, which lies in the Sarno River valley between Naples and Salerno, and the Lattari and Picentini mountains, stretching down from the slopes of Vesuvius. This means a happy marriage between volcanic soil and a good water supply, providing perfect conditions for growing crops.

For more than two centuries after its arrival in Europe, the tomato was considered an ornamental plant, and only in the eighteenth century did it become widely and popularly accepted in cooking. Under Bourbon rule, the tomato became revered as an anointed prince of cuisine. In Naples, it became a source of nourishment suitable for kings and farmers alike, until it reached its present celebrity status in the typical Mediterranean diet.

Campania was one of the first areas in Italy to cultivate and process the tomato, which is characteristically dubbed 'red gold' and is spread throughout virtually every corner of our region. The San Marzano is, however, mostly grown in the fertile soil of the Agro Nocerino-Sarnese. This particular variety of tomato is known and valued all over the world for its flavour and texture, which are enhanced when it is processed into tinned peeled tomatoes. It has a typically sweet but tart flavour, an elongated shape and a flesh with few seeds or fibres. When fully ripe, this pulpy tomato is bright red in colour and has a skin that is easily peeled off. Rich in flavour and nutritional value, it contains lycopene, beta-carotene, vitamin C, potassium and sodium, as well possessing antioxidant properties.

Today, thanks to the fact that San Marzano tomatoes have been granted PDO status by the European Union, Campania can be justly proud of the unique flavour of this fruit, which is such an integral and defining element of its traditional dishes. There is a very strong bond between the San Marzano tomato and its land of origin. The people of Campania, with its volcanic soil and sunny temperate Mediterranean climate, prize the San Marzano not only as their very own variety of tomato, but also because of its now widespread commercial cultivation. On the small independent farms with their small lots of land scattered across the landscape, nature and tradition have given rise to an unbeatable combination of climate, sea and history.

PASTA

When talking about the sun and heaven-blessed combinations, it would be difficult not to mention the pivotal role of pasta. It was during the nineteenth century that the making and eating of pasta became widespread in Campania, as demonstrated by the several pasta makers who began their activity at Torre Annunziata, Torre del Greco and Nola. The latter used to produce more than 200 kinds of 'short' and 'long' pasta. Whatever the much debated origins of pasta may be, it has an undeniably Neapolitan character, both as the main ingredient in the

Mediterranean diet and as a cultural expression. Pasta is in fact an element recurrently found in Neapolitan art and literature, and today the majority of the 180 Italian pasta companies are based in Campania.

Pasta is made of two basic and extremely simple ingredients: durum wheat flour and water. The first stage in the processing of the dough is called *granolatura* (kneading) and gives homogeneity to the product. Subsequently the dough is shaped through a process known as *trafilatura* (moulding); this is still done by hand, using bronze *trafilati* (wirework moulds) to obtain the pasta shape desired.

A fundamental part of the whole process is the drying stage, which is meticulously monitored. In Campania's pasta factories, drying is carried out at a temperature of 38°C and lasts between 24 and 36 hours, whereas this is done much faster in large-scale industrial production. According to a Campanian tradition, a good pasta has to 'stand' during the cooking process. In other words, it must contain a sufficiently high level of gluten, the protein which keeps the flour together and prevents the pasta disintegrating while cooking. These characteristics are enhanced by the slower methods used by Neapolitan pasta makers.

EXEMPLARY FRUITS

Campania is renowned for the cultivation of fruit, including apricots, apples and lemons of very high quality. Lemon trees, first introduced by the Arabs, cling almost miraculously to the terraced fields that characterize the Neapolitan and Amalfi coast. One of the reasons why lemons grow so well and with such a wonderful flavour is the technique of using so-called *pagliarelle* (straw mats), which are put over the foliage of the trees and supported by wooden posts in order to protect the plant from the cold and coastal winds – an ancient technique necessary during the coldest months of the year.

The Sorrento Pensinsula and the island of Procida, in particular, yield lemons of a superior quality that are renowned all over the world for their taste and aroma. The skin, rich in essential oils, is used to flavour creams and ice creams, and to enhance the taste of certain traditional regional dishes. These are also the lemons, along with those grown on Capri, that are used to make the famous *limoncello* liqueur.

Olive oil, tomatoes, mozzarella and other dairy products, pasta, wines and spirits: these products are combined in Neapolitan cuisine to create a perfect harmony of flavours, representing a synthesis of tradition, culture and land. All these and more are drawn from the lands of Campania to make up a cuisine that honours simple ingredients, satisfies the appetite and soothes the soul with its lighthearted use of the best that nature has to offer.

ANTIPASTI, ZUPPE E MINESTRE

Appetizers & soups

COZZE AL PEPE
Peppered mussels

The simplicity of this typical fishermen's dish from the Borgo Marinari area of Naples belies the delicious results. The village of Borgo Marinari, just outside the fortress walls of the Castel dell'Ovo in Santa Lucia, Naples' ancient fishing quarter, was long home to fishermen who drew their daily catch from the Bay of Naples. A steaming bowl of these mussels will prove irresistible to anyone who loves this particular seafood – or to any seafood lover at all.

✢ SERVES 4

1 kg (2¹⁄₄ lb) fresh mussels
plenty of freshly ground black pepper
lemon wedges, to serve

Rinse the mussels in plenty of changes of cold water to remove any sand or grit, then scrub and remove the beards. Tap each mussel on the work surface and discard any that do not close or which have broken shells. Put the mussels in a large heavy saucepan, cover the pan and cook over a high heat for a few minutes until the shells open. Alternatively, cook the mussels over a hot grill or griddle pan.

When all the shells are open fully (discard any mussels that do not open), add lots of black pepper and stir for a minute or so. (Be careful not to overcook – otherwise the mussels will be rubbery.) Serve immediately with lemon wedges and perhaps some fresh, crusty bread.

CALAMARI E GAMBERONI AL PROFUMO DI MARE

Pan-fried squid & king prawns

Profumo di mare means 'perfume of the sea', and evokes the essence of this dish, which originated in the convents of Campania, born out of the Church's long tradition of providing food and shelter in these institutions. As with all Neapolitan recipes, choose the freshest and best-quality ingredients that you can find. The entire region of Campania is renowned for the quality of its produce, and this is reflected in the approach to food and cooking in general.

✣ SERVES 4

3 tablespoons olive oil
1 garlic clove, finely chopped
800 g (1³/₄ lb) fresh squid, cleaned
  and cut into rings (see note)
12 cherry tomatoes, halved
8–12 fresh raw king prawns, unpeeled
200 g (7 oz) mixed fresh shellfish
  such as mussels and clams, scrubbed
  and cleaned (see page 42)
salt and freshly ground black pepper
generous handful of fresh flat-leaf
  parsley, leaves picked and chopped,
  to garnish

Heat the oil in a large heavy frying pan over a medium heat. Sweat the garlic for 2–3 minutes until soft and translucent. Add the squid and sweat for a few more minutes, being careful not to scorch the garlic. Tip in the cherry tomatoes and cook for 15 minutes, until the tomatoes break down and soften. Finally, add the unpeeled king prawns and the shellfish. Stir through, then continue cooking over a medium heat for a further 5 minutes, shaking the pan occasionally. Season with salt and black pepper, sprinkle with plenty of parsley and serve immediately with slices of hot toasted bread such as crostini or ciabatta (rubbed with a cut piece of garlic and drizzled with a little extra virgin olive oil, then toasted).

Cleaning and preparing squid Clean and prepare the fresh squid by pulling the tentacles away from the body and removing the quill inside. Discard. Rinse the squid under cold running water, including the tentacles, then trim away the excess membrane at either side of the body and peel away the skin. Remove the tentacles, ink sac and beak. Slice into rings or squares. When cutting squares, if you score the flesh lightly with a knife in a crisscross pattern, taking care not to cut the flesh all the way through, the squid will curl nicely when cooked.

MOZZARELLA IN CARROZZA
Mozzarella in a carriage

The name of this traditional Neapolitan speciality sums up these fantastic little sandwiches – the bread that forms the 'carriage' encases meltingly hot mozzarella in a crisp shell for transportation to your mouth. Ideal as a snack as well as an appetizer, they make the most of their simple ingredients and will not last long on the plate.

✤ SERVES 4–6

24 slices day-old crusty white bread
  such as ciabatta
12 slices buffalo mozzarella or
  fior di latte cheese, about 1 cm
  (1/2 in) thick each
3 eggs
60–90 ml (2–3 fl oz) milk
light olive oil for shallow-frying
salt and freshly ground black pepper
plain flour for dredging

Cut the bread to roughly the same size as the mozzarella slices, allowing a little extra around the edge for the cheese to spread. Sandwich each slice of mozzarella between 2 slices of bread, pressing down lightly around the edges of each one to 'seal'. Whisk the eggs with the milk until fluffy, and season with salt and black pepper.

Heat enough oil for shallow-frying (depending on the thickness of your sandwiches) in a heavy frying pan over a medium heat. Dredge each of the little sandwiches in flour to coat lightly, then dip in the beaten egg, allowing the bread to soak up the eggy mixture. Carefully lower the sandwiches into the very hot oil, cooking a few at a time. Be careful not to crowd the pan, as the temperature of the oil will drop and your sandwiches will end up soggy, rather than being crisp and light. Allow to cook for a few minutes until the cheese starts to melt and the bread is crisp and golden underneath. Using a spatula or egg slice, turn the sandwiches over and press down slightly with the spatula to flatten. Cook on the other side for another 2–3 minutes, then remove and drain on kitchen paper.

These sandwiches are best piping hot and fresh from the pan, so serve immediately – with a warning about the hot melted cheese inside.

Variations If you like, make a paste out of 3 or 4 large anchovy fillets stored in oil, and spread evenly over one side of the sandwiches before topping with the mozzarella. Alternatively, add the finely chopped leaves of a few sprigs of fresh oregano or thyme to the egg mixture used to coat the bread.

CARCIOFI CON MOZZARELLA
Baked artichokes stuffed with mozzarella

It is best to choose young, tender artichokes for this simple Neapolitan recipe. Look for the small purple-tinged ones, which have barely any choke at all, in spring and early summer – although obviously you need to make sure you pick ones large enough to stuff. If you cannot find baby artichokes, choose the most tender, juicy ones available. (The larger the artichokes, the tougher they will be.) The juices will keep the artichokes moist as they bake, and the leaves will be deliciously soft, pulling off easily as you eat them with their melting mozzarella stuffing

+ SERVES 4

12 young, tender globe artichokes or 8 medium artichokes (depending on the season)

juice of 1 lemon

6 small balls of buffalo mozzarella cheese, about 150 g (5 oz) in total, chopped

4 tablespoons freshly grated Parmesan cheese

4 tablespoons good-quality dried breadcrumbs (see note)

2 eggs, beaten

scant 1 tablespoon olive oil plus extra for drizzling

salt and freshly ground black pepper

Preheat the oven to 180°C (350°F/Gas 4). Cut off the artichoke stems – you need to trim them right off so that you can stand the artichokes in the baking dish for cooking. Next trim about 2 cm (1 in) off the tops of the artichokes, then snap off any tough outer leaves (if necessary, trim the tops of the larger leaves using a pair of scissors). Leave to soak for 30 minutes in a glass or ceramic bowl of cold water with the lemon juice added – make sure that the artichokes are covered, to prevent discoloration. Drain, then scrape out and discard the fuzzy choke using a teaspoon and pull out any prickly inner leaves – the younger the artichokes, the less choke you will have to deal with. If you are using larger artichokes with very tightly packed leaves, you may need to blanch them in boiling water for a few minutes to soften slightly and loosen the leaves. Drain and set aside while you make the filling.

Put the mozzarella, Parmesan, breadcrumbs, eggs and the scant 1 tablespoon olive oil in a bowl. Season well with salt and black pepper. Mix the ingredients together well with a fork, and use the filling to stuff the artichokes. Using a spoon, push down the stuffing between the leaves as well as generously filling the centre of each artichoke. Stand the artichokes in a single layer in an oiled baking dish or baking tray with shallow sides, add a little water and drizzle with a little extra oil.

Bake in the preheated oven for about 45 minutes until tender, basting the artichokes frequently with any juices in the pan. Keep an eye on them and be careful not to overcook them; otherwise they will dry out. (Smaller artichokes will need less cooking time.) Serve immediately, while still piping hot.

Note It is easy to make your own dried breadcrumbs. Simply use up any leftover good-quality stale bread such as ciabatta or sourdough. Whizz into medium-coarse breadcrumbs in a food processor, chop up with a knife or break up with your hands. Spread the breadcrumbs on a flat baking sheet, and leave in the oven at a very low heat until they are dried and toasty. (The ideal time to make them is after you have used the oven for something else – you can then utilize any residual heat to dry out the bread.) Use straight away or store in an airtight jar until needed. They should keep for up to 2 weeks.

OLIVE OIL

Like wine, extra virgin olive oil has been blessed with something of a renaissance in Campania, especially in relation to mono-cultivar olive oils (oil pressed from a single cultivar of olive tree from a single estate) and organically produced oils.

Olive oil was introduced to Campania by the Romans, who subsidized its production. Olive groves and estates, and hence olive oil production, spread virtually over the whole region but with a particular concentration in the Cilento area and on the Sorrento Peninsula. The Campanian tradition of making olive oil is among the most advanced to be found in the Mediterranean basin, where most of the world's olive production is based. The European Union has given Protected Designation of Origin (PDO) to two types of extra virgin olive oil produced in the Campania region, Olio Extra Vergine d'Oliva del Cilento and Olio Extra Vergine d'Oliva della Penisola Sorrentina, in order to safeguard their indisputable high quality.

These olive oils are highly prized, obtained from the first pressing of the fruits and produced from olive tree species native to Campania that have been cultivated since ancient times. They are rich in vitamins A, D and E, and are characterized by low acidity and the presence of unsaturated fats. The benefits of olive oil in helping to prevent and control high levels of cholesterol are now widely known. Yet there was a time when the Neapolitan diet was considered very unhealthy because of the widespread use of this oil. How times change.

There are approximately 700 olive oil producers based in Campania. In a highly competitive global market, the quality and integrity of the product are key factors for success. With excellent raw materials at their disposal, small- and medium-sized olive oil producers in Campania have created a great product by monitoring quality at every stage of production and by adhering to the long-standing regional traditions that govern the making of olive oil in the region. Rather than being left behind by an increasingly mechanized agricultural world driven primarily by economic considerations, they have turned their artisan-like approach to the making of this traditional product very much to their advantage. Campanian extra virgin olive oil is becoming an increasingly competitive product on both domestic and foreign markets, drawing staunch devotees because of its high quality and flavour.

GNOCCHETTI E COZZE IN BRODETTO
Gnocchetti sardi & mussel soup

Gnocchetti sardi, slightly smaller than ordinary dried gnocchi, are also made with semolina flour. In this typical soup from Naples' Chiaia neighbourhood, it is paired with fresh mussels to make a robust dish with clean flavours. Chiaia's origins lie in the seventeenth and eighteenth centuries with the Spanish, but today it plays host to high-end boutiques and Naples' hottest nightclubs.

✣ SERVES 4

1.25 kg (3¼ lb) fresh mussels
2 tablespoons olive oil
1 garlic clove, finely chopped
1 fresh red chilli pepper, deseeded and
  finely chopped
250 g (9 oz) ripe cherry tomatoes,
  chopped
250 g (9 oz) gnocchetti sardi
  or similar-shaped dried pasta such
  as orechiette
salt and freshly ground black pepper
handful of fresh flat-leaf parsley,
  leaves picked and chopped

Rinse the mussels in plenty of cold water to remove any grit, then scrub and remove the beards. Tap each mussel on a work surface and discard any that do not close or which have broken shells. Heat the oil in a pan over a medium heat and sauté the garlic and chilli for a few minutes until soft and starting to colour. Remove the garlic and chilli using a slotted spoon; discard.

Add the tomatoes to the garlic/chilli-infused oil in the pan, and cook for about 10 minutes. Add the mussels, cover, and cook over a medium-high heat until they open, shaking the pan frequently and stirring with a wooden spoon. When all the mussels have opened (discard any that remain closed), remove the pan from the heat. Leave to cool slightly, remove the shells and return the mussel flesh to the tomato sauce.

In the meantime, cook the gnocchetti for half the recommended cooking time in a large pan of slightly salted boiling water. Drain and add to the mussels with a little of the cooking liquid – the soup should be a little liquidy, but not too watery. Return the pan to a medium heat, season the soup with salt and black pepper, and cook for a few minutes. Sprinkle with chopped parsley and serve hot, with lots of freshly toasted bread to mop up the juices.

MINESTRA DI SCAROLE E FAGIOLI
White bean & escarole soup

Minestre are made with vegetables and meat, and are medium-thick like a broth or thick like the more well known minestrone, which usually contains pasta or rice. Very much from the *cucina povera* tradition, *minestre* have all the gusto of lots of traditional Italian soups and make a meal in themselves. They are often served topped with a grating of Parmesan cheese.

⊹ SERVES 4

500 g (1 lb 2 oz) dried cannellini
 beans
pinch of bicarbonate of soda
1 garlic clove, peeled but left whole,
 plus 1 extra, finely chopped
1 celery stick
4 bunches of escarole, roughly
 chopped
100 g (3¹/₂ oz) pancetta or fat bacon,
 diced
2 tablespoons olive oil
salt and freshly ground black pepper

Soak the beans overnight in plenty of cold water with a pinch of bicarbonate of soda. Rinse well and put in a large heavy saucepan. Cover with 1.5 litres (2³/4 pints) water and bring to the boil (do not add salt, as this toughens the skins). Add the whole garlic clove and the celery, cover the pan and simmer over a low heat for about 50 minutes or until the beans are cooked, but still with a slight bite, skimming off any scum that rises to the surface.

Just before the end of the cooking time, blanch the escarole in salted boiling water until just wilted. Drain well. Meanwhile, heat the oil in a deep-sided heavy frying pan over a medium heat. Add the escarole, pancetta or fat bacon and extra chopped garlic. Sweat for about 5 minutes until the pancetta is cooked and the garlic has softened. Remove the whole garlic and celery from the beans; discard. Add the beans with a little of their cooking liquid – just enough to make a medium-thick soup – to the pan. Season with salt and black pepper. Simmer gently for a further 15 minutes. Serve hot.

ZUPPA DI FAGIOLI
Cannellini bean soup

The combination of cannellini beans and basil may seem like a slightly unusual one, but it gives this traditional bean soup from the Campanian countryside a deliciously fresh flavour.

⊹ SERVES 4

600 g (1 lb 5 oz) shelled fresh
 cannellini beans
100 ml (3¹/₂ fl oz) olive oil
2 celery sticks, roughly chopped
3 garlic cloves
2 or 3 large fresh basil leaves
2 or 3 sprigs of fresh flat-leaf parsley,
 leaves picked and finely chopped
salt and freshly ground black pepper
freshly made croûtons, to serve

Put the beans in a pot (preferably clay) with 1.75 litres (3 pints) cold water, cover and bring to the boil. Reduce the heat to low and cook very gently for 2 hours. Just before the end of the cooking time, heat the oil in a pan over a medium heat. Add the celery, garlic and basil. Cover and leave to sweat for about 5 minutes until soft. Add to the beans with just enough water to make a thick soup. Season with salt and black pepper. Serve hot, with croûtons scattered over the top of each serving.

Fresh cannellini beans Unless you are lucky enough to live in the hills of Benevento and Avellino, for instance, where premium cannellini beans are grown, you may find fresh cannellini beans difficult to find. If so, substitute with dried ones, soaking and rinsing as usual before cooking.

ZUPPA DI FAGIOLI E SCAROLA
Bread soup with cannellini beans & escarole

A traditional dish from the countryside surrounding Naples, this hearty and warming soup contains cannellini beans and toasted bread to satisfy the appetite, while the tomatoes add a lightness and zest that stop it from being too heavy. Escarole is best for the soup, as it has a milder flavour than its more bitter relatives, Belgian and curly endive. The secret is to blanch it slightly before adding to the soup, so that it retains its bright green colour.

⚜ SERVES 4

400 g (14 oz) dried cannellini beans
pinch of bicarbonate of soda
2 garlic cloves, finely chopped
1 celery stick, chopped
125 g (4^1/$_2$ oz) crushed tomatoes
2 tablespoons olive oil
600 g (1 lb 6 oz) escarole, leaves
  separated and roughly chopped
8 thick slices of freshly toasted
  day-old Italian bread such as
  ciabatta or pane casereccio
generous handful of fresh flat-leaf
  parsley, leaves picked and chopped
salt and freshly ground black pepper

Soak the beans overnight in plenty of cold water with a pinch of bicarbonate of soda. Rinse well and transfer to a large heavy saucepan. Cover well with plenty of cold fresh water (about 1.25 litres/2 pints). Add the garlic, celery, tomatoes and oil. Season with salt and black pepper. Bring to the boil, then reduce the heat and simmer for about 50 minutes or until the beans still have a slight bite to them, rather than being mushy. Skim off any scum that rises to the surface as the beans cook.

Just before the beans are cooked, blanch the escarole in a separate saucepan of salted boiling water for a few minutes until it has just wilted. Drain and add to the beans. Check and adjust the seasoning if necessary. To serve, lay 2 slices of the toasted bread in the bottom of each of the serving bowls, ladle over the soup, sprinkle with the parsley and serve immediately.

ZUPPA DI FAVE SECCHE
Stewed broad beans

More of a side dish than a soup, this recipe originates from the region around Mount Vesuvius and makes a hearty winter dish. Dried broad beans are used here, but you can make a version with fresh broad beans when they are in season. Simply blanch in boiling water for a couple of minutes if necessary to loosen the skins, then slip the pods out of their skins before adding to the pan. Obviously you will also need a much shorter cooking time. Slow, gentle cooking, however, is still important – a fundamental part of so much Campanian regional cuisine.

✢ SERVES 4

500 g (1 lb 2 oz) dried broad beans
pinch of bicarbonate of soda
100 g (3¹/₂ oz) pancetta or fat bacon, diced
1 garlic clove, finely chopped
2 onions, finely chopped
1 litre (1³/₄ pints) hot water
about 2 tablespoons good-quality extra virgin olive oil
generous handful of fresh flat-leaf parsley, leaves picked and chopped
salt and freshly ground black pepper

Soak the beans in cold water overnight with a pinch of bicarbonate of soda. Melt the fat bacon or pancetta in a large pan over a medium heat and sweat the garlic and onions, but do not allow to brown. When the onions are soft and starting to caramelize, add half of the hot water and bring to the boil. Add the broad beans and cover with the remaining hot water. Return to the boil and continue cooking at this temperature for 10 minutes.

Reduce the heat to low, skim off any scum from the surface and season with salt and black pepper. Cook, covered, over a very gentle heat for about 4 hours until the beans are barely tender, taking care that they do not catch on the bottom of the pan. Check the seasoning, then transfer to a serving dish. Serve hot, drizzled with the olive oil and sprinkled with plenty of chopped parsley.

ZUPPA DI PATATE E CARCIOFI
Potato & artichoke soup

Potatoes and artichokes make a good pairing, and the slow cooking in this classic Neapolitan recipe ensures that their textures meld together for a harmonious balance and satisfying flavour.

✢ SERVES 4

1 kg (2¹/₄ lb) floury potatoes
6 fresh artichokes
1 onion, finely chopped
500 g (1 lb 2 oz) fresh ripe tomatoes, preferably plum, chopped
2 tablespoons olive oil
2 teaspoons dried oregano
salt and freshly ground black pepper

Peel, rinse and chop the potatoes into 1-cm (¹/₂-in) dice. Rinse the artichokes, remove the tough outer leaves and cut into slices. Using a knife or a spoon, scrape off and discard any choke or prickly inner leaves. Put the potatoes and artichokes into a large heavy saucepan, and add the onion, tomatoes, oil and oregano. Cover with twice the depth of water, so that if your vegetables are 2.5 cm (1 in) deep, for instance, the water comes up to a depth of 5 cm (2 in). Season with salt and black pepper, and cook over a gentle heat for about an hour. Serve hot.

PASTA E RISO

Pasta & rice

MACCHERONCELLI ARRABBIATI
Maccheroncelli with tomato & chilli

Perhaps one of the best known of the *cucina povera* pasta sauces, *arrabbiati* is traditionally made with *ciccioli,* or pork scratchings – no part of a beast was wasted, and cheap cuts were always used to their best advantage. Two other fundamental ingredients in this spicy sauce are tomatoes and chilli; it is the latter that gives the sauce its name – *arrabbiato* means 'angry' in Italian.

✢ SERVES 4

500 g (1 lb 2 oz) maccheroncelli
  such as bucatini or ziti, broken up
  into pieces, or shorter dried tubular
  pasta such as penne rigate
50 g (2 oz) lard or olive oil
1 onion, finely chopped
100 g (3¹/₂ oz) pancetta or speck or
  ciccioli (pork scratchings), diced
300 g (10 oz) fresh ripe tomatoes,
  preferably plum, chopped
1 fresh red chilli, deseeded and
  finely chopped
freshly ground black pepper
freshly shaved or grated Parmesan
  cheese, to serve
freshly shaved or grated pecorino
  cheese, to serve

Bring a large pan of slightly salted water to the boil, and cook the pasta until al dente.

Meanwhile, melt the lard or heat the olive oil in a heavy frying pan over a medium-high heat. Add the onion and sweat for a few minutes until soft, then add the pancetta, speck or ciccioli along with the tomatoes and chilli. Season with black pepper. Cook for a few minutes, stirring all the time so the sauce does not catch. Drain the pasta, add to the sauce and stir through. Sprinkle with lots of grated Parmesan and pecorino, and serve immediately.

BUCATINI CON I PEPERONCINI
Bucatini with green peperoncini, tomatoes & basil

A classic *cucina povera* dish, this one features green *peperoncini*, small sweet peppers with a hint of heat that are sometimes known as Tuscan peppers or sweet Italian peppers. They are often pickled and sold in jars as an antipasto or for use in salads or as a garnish.

✤ SERVES 4

2 tablespoons olive oil

500 g (1 lb 2 oz) small green peperoncini (see note), deseeded and chopped

2 garlic cloves, finely chopped

500 g (1 lb 2 oz) tinned peeled whole plum tomatoes, chopped

3 or 4 large fresh basil leaves, torn into small pieces

500 g (1 lb 2 oz) bucatini (perciatelli) or similar long tubular pasta such as mezzanelli

Heat the oil in a frying pan over a medium heat. Add the *peperoncini* and sweat for a few minutes until soft. As soon as they are cooked, remove from the frying pan with a slotted spoon and set aside. Using the same oil, sweat the garlic for a couple of minutes until soft. Add the tomatoes and basil. Bring to a simmer, then reduce the heat and cook gently for 30 minutes. Return the *peperoncini* to the pan and keep the sauce warm.

Meanwhile, cook the bucatini in a large pan of slightly salted boiling water until al dente. Drain and serve topped with the tasty sauce.

Note The *peperoncini* used here are mildly hot, curved, sweet red chillies. They are usually picked when they are 5–7.5 cm (2–3 in) long. Mature red ones have slightly wrinkled skin and taper to a blunt lobed end; green *peperoncini* are the same variety picked before ripening. If you cannot find *peperoncini*, use another mild sweet pepper, or replace with sliced aubergine.

FUSILLI CON LA RICOTTA
Fusilli with ricotta, tomatoes & Parmesan

One of the by-products of buffalo mozzarella is buffalo ricotta. It has a more intense flavour than cow's milk ricotta and combines beautifully with the acidity of the tomatoes to make a smooth, creamy sauce. Don't worry if you cannot find buffalo ricotta; ordinary ricotta will work just as well.

✤ SERVES 4

2 tablespoons olive oil

1 small onion, finely chopped

1 kg (2¼ lb) tinned whole peeled plum tomatoes

400 g (14 oz) fusilli

250 g (9 oz) fresh ricotta cheese

1 tablespoon freshly grated Parmesan cheese, plus extra for serving

3 or 4 large fresh basil leaves, torn into small pieces

salt and freshly ground black pepper

Heat the oil in a pan over a medium heat and sweat the onion gently until soft and starting to caramelize. Reduce to a low heat, add the tomatoes and simmer very gently for 1 hour, breaking them up with a wooden spoon as they cook down. The longer you simmer the sauce, the tastier the tomatoes will be.

Cook the fusilli in a large pan of slightly salted boiling water until al dente. While the pasta is cooking, mix the ricotta with a ladleful of the cooking water. Add a little tomato sauce and grated Parmesan, and mix to a smooth cream. Drain the pasta and add the ricotta mixture and the remaining tomato sauce. Season with salt and black pepper. Mix well, sprinkle over the basil and extra grated Parmesan, and serve.

SALSA GENOVESE
Beef, onion & wine sauce

Despite the 'salsa' in the name, this is a classic *ragù*. It is also very Neapolitan in origin, rather than from Genoa, as the second half of the title implies. Debates on the origin of its name abound, but what is not in question is its place in the culinary heritage of Naples and its origins in the sixteenth century. The balance of ingredients has altered over the years, with a gradually increasing emphasis on onion and at one time, when Naples was not so affluent, much less meat. Now it is a dish that is often eaten on a Sunday; it is also one that can be served in two parts, as different courses. For the first course, the meat is removed from the sauce and set aside, and freshly cooked al dente pasta is added to the gently simmering sauce and mixed through. This is then served topped with a drizzle of extra virgin olive oil and a sprinkling of freshly shaved Parmesan cheese. The second course is made up of the meat, dressed in a little of the sauce, which is served with vegetable side dishes. The version here, however, uses minced beef, rather than a whole piece of meat that is later sliced, and works well on a bed of freshly cooked pasta.

✣ SERVES 4–6

3 tablespoons olive oil

2 tablespoons lard

600 g (1 lb 6 oz) onions, sliced
 into rings

500 g (1 lb 2 oz) lean beef mince

3 carrots, sliced

2 celery sticks, sliced

30 g (1 oz) salami napoli, diced

30 g (1 oz) prosciutto crudo or cured
 pork shoulder, diced

100 ml (3¹/₂ fl oz) passata

1 glass of dry white wine

salt and freshly ground black pepper

Heat the oil and lard in a large heavy saucepan over a medium heat. Add the onions and sweat for a few minutes until soft, then add the beef, carrots, celery, salami and prosciutto or cured pork shoulder. Cook, stirring and breaking up the beef with a wooden spoon, until the meat has browned. Dilute the passata with a little warm water and add to the pan. When the liquid has reduced completely, pour over the wine and leave the sauce to simmer gently, covered, for at least 2 hours.

Just before serving, mash down the sauce with a fork until the onions are smooth. Serve hot with al dente pasta such as rigatoni or paccheri.

PENNETTE PRIMAVERA
Pasta with spring vegetables

Courgettes are at their best when young and small, and those are the ones you should be looking to use in this quintessential springtime dish from the *cucina povera* tradition. Choose courgettes with firm skins, making sure to avoid the larger ones, which will be filled with seeds and watery.

❖ SERVES 4

300 g (10 oz) courgettes
a little olive oil
2 hard-boiled eggs, chopped
400 g (14 oz) pennette such as penne rigate or similar
about 50 g (1³/4 oz) butter, cut into small pieces
freshly grated Parmesan cheese
salt and freshly ground black pepper
fresh mint leaves, to serve

Top and tail the courgettes and halve lengthways. Cut into strips. Heat a little olive oil in a pan over a medium-high heat, and sauté the courgettes for a few minutes until golden brown. Season with salt and black pepper, then transfer to a serving bowl with the chopped eggs.

Meanwhile, cook the pennette in a large saucepan of slightly salted boiling water until al dente. Drain and transfer with a little of the cooking water (just enough to keep the pasta moist) to the bowl with the courgettes and eggs. Stir in a generous amount of butter and grated Parmesan, mixing thoroughly but gently, so that you do not break up the eggs too much. Garnish with the mint leaves and sprinkle over plenty of black pepper, before serving straight away.

SPAGHETTI AL FILETTO DI POMODORO
Spaghetti with tomatoes & basil

When you think of the classic tomato sauce for spaghetti, this is the recipe that should top your list. You can also use it as a base when a recipe calls for tomato sauce as one of the ingredients.

❖ SERVES 4

2 tablespoons olive oil
2 garlic cloves, finely chopped
400 g (14 oz) tinned peeled whole plum tomatoes, drained, deseeded and chopped, or 400 g (14 oz) fresh plum tomatoes, peeled, deseeded and chopped (see page 116)
generous handful of fresh basil leaves, finely sliced
pinch of sugar
salt
400 g (14 oz) spaghetti

Heat the oil in a pan over a medium heat and sweat the garlic for a few minutes until soft and starting to caramelize. Add the tomatoes, half of the basil and a pinch of sugar. Season with salt, and simmer over a gentle heat for at least 15 minutes.

Cook the spaghetti in a large pan of slightly salted boiling water until al dente. Drain and mix with the sauce. Sprinkle the remaining basil over the top and serve immediately.

Note When using tinned tomatoes, always buy whole peeled plum tomatoes; they are more flavourful and better quality than those sold already chopped. Adding sugar to the sauce not only cuts the acidity of the tomato, but also helps to bring out its flavour. This works particularly well when you are using fresh tomatoes (as you can in this dish if you like).

PASTA E CECI
Pasta & chickpeas

Pasta mista and dried chickpeas combine in this warm, hearty dish that shows its country roots in its rustic nature and use of pulses. Simplicity is key, and this nourishing dish will banish the chill – and your hunger – on a cold winter's day.

✣ SERVES 4

250 g (9 oz) dried chickpeas
pinch of bicarbonate of soda
300 g (10 oz) pasta mista or raganelle
2 tablespoons olive oil
1–2 garlic cloves, finely chopped
2 teaspoons chopped fresh
  oregano leaves
handful of fresh flat-leaf parsley,
  leaves picked and chopped
salt and freshly ground black pepper

Soak the chickpeas overnight in plenty of cold water with a pinch of bicarbonate of soda. Rinse well and transfer to a heavy saucepan. Cover well with fresh water, and bring to the boil over a medium heat. Do not add salt initially, as this toughen the skins. Reduce the heat and simmer for about 3 hours until the beans are tender but still have a slight bite. Season with the oil, garlic, oregano, salt and black pepper, and keep on a gentle simmer.

Cook the pasta for half its cooking time in a large pan of slightly salted boiling water. Drain and add to the chickpeas. When the pasta is cooked al dente, transfer the pasta and chickpeas to a serving dish, sprinkle with the parsley and serve immediately.

PASTA E LENTICCHIE
Pasta & lentils

Lentils are a good source of iron, and also contain important nutrients such as calcium and vitamins A and B. In Campania, particularly in the remote and mountainous rural areas, where meat was not always available, beans and pulses became an important addition to the diet. They were used to make tasty, filling dishes that could be eaten over the winter months, as demonstrated in this simple dish from the region around Mount Vesuvius.

✣ SERVES 4

300 g (10 oz) brown lentils such as
  Puy, picked and rinsed
2 garlic cloves, crushed
2 tablespoons olive oil
3 tinned whole peeled plum tomatoes
2 or 3 sprigs of fresh flat-leaf parsley,
  leaves picked and chopped
400 g (14 oz) tubetti
salt and freshly ground black pepper

Put the lentils into a saucepan and cover with plenty of cold water. Cover the pan with a lid, and cook over a low heat for 1½ hours until soft. Add the garlic, oil, tomatoes and parsley, and season with salt and black pepper. Continue cooking for a further 30 minutes.

Cook the pasta in a large pan of slightly salted boiling water for half its cooking time. Drain and add to the lentils, and continue cooking until the pasta is al dente. Leave to stand for 5 minutes before serving.

SPAGHETTI ALLA CAPRESE
Spaghetti with tuna, anchovies, tomatoes & olives

The ingredients used in this spaghetti recipe are typical of those found in dishes cooked in family kitchens on the island of Capri. Tuna, anchovies, tomatoes and olives crop up in different combinations in various other dishes from Campania. They may all have strong flavours, but they work well together to provide a wonderful gutsy taste explosion.

✢ SERVES 4

4 tablespoons olive oil
500 g (1 lb 2 oz) tinned whole peeled
   plum tomatoes
1 x 200-g (7-oz) jar tuna in oil,
   drained
50 g (1³/₄ oz) salted anchovy fillets,
   chopped
50 g (1³/₄ oz) Gaeta or similar black
   olives, pitted and halved
100 g (3¹/₂ oz) buffalo mozzarella,
   finely diced
400 g (14 oz) spaghetti
salt and freshly ground black pepper

Heat 2 tablespoons of the oil in a pan over a medium heat and add the tomatoes. Simmer gently for 10 minutes until the sauce has thickened. Season with salt and black pepper.

In a separate pan, heat the remaining 2 tablespoons of oil over a medium heat. Add the tuna and use a wooden spoon to break it up into flakes. Add the anchovies and olives, and stir through. Now add the finely diced mozzarella to the thickened tomato sauce.

Cook the spaghetti in a large pan of slightly salted boiling water until al dente. Drain and mix with the tuna sauce. Transfer to a serving dish and add the tomato and mozzarella sauce. Mix through gently and serve immediately.

SPAGHETTI ALLA ROSINELLA
Spaghetti with prawns, squid & clams

In this typical pasta dish from the Posillipo district of Naples, the most is made of the fresh seafood available along the coast of Campania. Posillipo, situated at the western end of the Bay of Naples and leading down to the water, is one of the oldest areas in the city – references to it can be found in both classical Greek and Roman works. Today, it is very much a residential quarter, but glimpses of its early history can be found in the Roman ruins at the water's edge. There are also remains of the villa complex of Roman equestrian and contemporary of Emperor Augustus, Vedius Pollius, including an amphitheatre perched on the cliffs above the bay.

✢ SERVES 4

2 tablespoons olive oil
2 garlic cloves, finely chopped
1 fresh red chilli, deseeded and
  finely chopped
300 g (10 oz) fresh clams, scrubbed
  and rinsed well (see note)
2 fresh squid, cleaned and prepared,
  cut into rings or small squares (see
  note on page 16)
200–250 g (7–8 oz) fresh raw prawns,
  peeled and deveined
400 g (14 oz) spaghetti
salt and freshly ground black pepper
fresh flat-leaf parsley, chopped,
  to serve

Heat the oil in a large pan over a medium heat, and sweat the garlic and chilli for a few minutes until soft. Tap the clams on a work surface and discard any that do not close. Add the clams and squid to the pan with half of the garlic and half of the chilli, and continue to sweat, taking care that the garlic and chilli do not scorch. As soon as the clams open (discard any that do not), tip the contents of the pan onto a plate and set aside. Add the prawns to the same pan with the remaining garlic and chilli, and sauté over a medium-high heat for a few minutes until cooked. Pick the flesh from the clam shells, discard the shells and return the flesh to the pan with the squid, garlic and chilli. (If you prefer, you can keep the clams in their shells for serving.) Season with salt and a little black pepper, and toss to heat through.

Meanwhile, cook the spaghetti in a large pan of slightly salted boiling water until al dente. Drain and add to the sauce with a tiny amount of the cooking water (just enough to keep the pasta moist). Stir through well, transfer to a large serving bowl or individual pasta bowls, and sprinkle with lots of chopped parsley. Serve immediately.

Preparing clams Tap the clams on a work surface and discard any that do not close. Scrub the clams well under cold running water to wash away any grit. If you are not using farmed clams, you may need to purge them of sand or grit, but a good scrub on the outside and proper rinsing should do the trick in either case. Otherwise, put the clams in a large bowl of salted water, making sure they are well covered (but do not cover the bowl). Soak in the refrigerator for a couple of hours or even overnight – any grit or sand will be left behind in the bottom of the bowl when you remove the clams. Rinse in plenty of fresh cold water, then strain the water through a fine cloth such as muslin or a clean dishcloth. You then pick out your clams and discard the grit. (Or you could simply rinse under cold running water.)

MOZZARELLA DI BUFALA

At Campania Felix, situated on the plains of the Caserta province between Francolise and Grazzanize, the family have been making *mozzarella di bufala*, or buffalo mozzarella, for more than 100 years. And it is more than simply a business to them – it's an operation that still very much reflects the ethos of founder Enrico Parente, who said in 1919: 'Only buffalo milk, milk enzymes, rennet and salt. These are the only ingredients to produce my mozzarella. High-quality mozzarella! On my word of honour.'

They can guarantee the quality of their product because they own the herd of buffalo, and the entire process from milking to finished cheese takes only 12 hours. The animals are milked at four in the morning. The milk is instantly pasteurized, then a natural fermenting agent is added to encourage it to curdle. Curds are separated from the whey, and the whey is made into ricotta. The remaining curd is salted, shredded and cooled to make the mozzarella base. This is then placed in boiling water and stirred to melt it. Pieces are pulled off by hand either to make the familiar mozzarella balls or to be stretched into plaits. The balls and plaits are packed in slightly salted water to keep them fresh. The cheese is ready to be shipped at four in the afternoon.

The evident passion for making mozzarella – and its by-product ricotta, as well as other regional cheeses such as

caciocavallo and *provola affumicata* – is far from restricted to the people at Campania Felix, or to the province of Caserta. *Mozzarella di bufala campana* is highly prized and considered the true gem of Campania; it is certainly distinctly the region's own, and is increasingly gaining recognition in a demanding European market, as well as an ever-growing global one.

Although *mozzarella di bufala campana* has been made for hundreds of years (the water buffalo was introduced to Italy more than a thousand years ago), it is only in the past century or so that this cheese has been made as a commercial product. Today, the production chain involved in making and selling *mozzarella di bufala* is crucially important to the agricultural and wider economy of the region, where more than 400 independent dairy companies operate. In recognition of this, Campania's buffalo mozzarella was granted PDO (Protected Designation of Origin) status in 1996, a mark of authenticity and quality.

Buffalo mozzarella should not be confused with *fior di latte*, which is made in a similar fashion but from cow's milk. Although delicious, it lacks buffalo mozzarella's characteristic tang and has a lower fat and protein content.

VERMICELLI CON SUGO DI POLIPI
Vermicelli with octopus sauce

Although some people think of octopus as being tough, this really should not be the case. All it takes is a little care in the cooking – some octopus, some tomatoes, a little garlic, a little oil and a little slow-cooking. Once again, the approach in this dish from the Borgo Marinari is very much about the Neapolitan attitude of treating your ingredients with respect.

✢ SERVES 4

500 g (1 lb 2 oz) small octopus, rinsed
500 g (1 lb 2 oz) ripe tomatoes,
  peeled and deseeded
2 garlic cloves, crushed
about 2 tablespoons olive oil
600 g (1 lb 6 oz) vermicelli
salt and freshly ground black pepper
chopped fresh flat-leaf parsley,
  to serve

Put the octopus, tomatoes, garlic and oil in a terracotta or similar flameproof casserole dish. Season with salt and black pepper. Cover the dish with foil, then put on the lid (alternatively, you can use a pressure cooker). Cook over a gentle heat for about 30 minutes until the sauce turns a very dark colour.

Just before the sauce is ready, cook the vermicelli in a large pan of slightly salted boiling water until al dente. Drain and add to the sauce. Stir through, sprinkle generously with the parsley and serve immediately.

Tip Do not worry if you cannot find fresh octopus where you live; frozen octopus serves just as well and in many ways is as good as fresh because it is cleaned and frozen immediately, rather than facing a journey to the market or fishmonger.

FARFALLE CON TONNO E PISELLI
Farfalle with tuna & peas

The Sorrento peninsula is dotted with citrus groves and olive trees, and is a rich source of both produce and culinary inspiration – lemons, walnuts, pasta, cheese and dairy products, fish and seafood. The recipe here is typical of family recipes found along this enchanting coastline.

✢ SERVES 4

2 tablespoons olive oil
1 onion, finely chopped
350 g (12 oz) shelled fresh or frozen
  green peas
1 x 200-g (7-oz) jar tuna in oil,
  drained
400 g (14 oz) farfalle
generous handful of fresh flat-leaf
  parsley, chopped
salt and freshly ground black pepper

Heat the oil in a pan over a medium heat. Add the onion and sweat for a few minutes until soft and transparent. Add the peas and 250 ml (8 fl oz) water. Season with salt and black pepper. Cover and leave to simmer for about 15 minutes. Using a fork, break the tuna up into largish flakes and add to the peas. Continue cooking for a few more minutes.

Meanwhile, cook the pasta in a large pan of slightly salted boiling water until al dente. Drain, add to the sauce and stir through. Sprinkle over the chopped parsley and serve immediately.

LINGUINE CON VONGOLE E POMODORI
Linguine with clams & tomatoes

Clams are highly prized along the Campanian coastline. This dish comes from Naples' Borgo Marinari area, the source of many recipes that take advantage of the region's harvest from the sea.

✢ SERVES 4

1 kg (2¹/₄ lb) clams, scrubbed and
  cleaned (see note on page 42)
2 tablespoons olive oil
1 garlic clove, finely chopped
500 g (1 lb 2 oz) ripe tomatoes,
  peeled and deseeded (see page 116)
a couple of small crabs (optional)
600 g (1 lb 5 oz) linguine
handful of fresh flat-leaf parsley,
  leaves picked and chopped
salt and freshly ground black pepper

Put the clams in a heavy saucepan. Add a little water, cover the pan and steam over a medium-high heat until the shells open (discard any that do not). Remove the flesh and discard the shells. Heat the oil in a heavy frying pan over a medium heat. Sauté the clam flesh and garlic for a few minutes until the garlic is soft and starting to colour. Add the tomatoes and season with salt. Stir through and cook for another few minutes until the tomato starts to break down.

Pour the sauce into a flameproof clay pot or casserole, and simmer over a medium heat for about 15 minutes. Crush the crabs, if using, with a mortar and pestle, and put in a tightly bound cloth bag or piece of muslin. Plunge into the sauce while it is cooking. Leave for a few minutes to release the flavour, then discard.

Cook the linguine in a large pan of slightly salted boiling water until al dente. Drain, add to the sauce and stir through. Serve with a sprinkling of freshly ground black pepper and chopped parsley.

BUCATINI ALLA 'SETTEMBRINI'
Tricolour pasta

The three colours in this pasta dish represent the colours of the Italian flag. Simple but filling, it makes the perfect dish to serve for a lunch with friends and family. It is easy to increase the quantities if you want to serve more people.

❖ SERVES 4–6

1 kg (2¹/4 lb) bucatini or similar dried
   pasta such as fettuccine or linguine
300 g (10 oz) courgettes, cut into
   julienne or slices
1 garlic clove, finely chopped
   (optional)
150 g (5 oz) butter
1 quantity tomato sauce (see note
   at right and Spaghetti al filetto di
   pomodoro on page 37)
150 g (5 oz) Parmesan cheese, grated
salt and freshly ground black pepper

Cook the pasta in a large pan of slightly salted water until al dente; drain, reserving a little of the cooking liquid. Meanwhile, blanch the courgettes in boiling water for 30 seconds; drain. Sauté the courgettes and garlic, if using, in half the butter in a heavy frying pan over a medium heat for a few minutes. Season with salt and black pepper. Melt the remaining butter.

Arrange the pasta on three serving dishes or in a three-section rectangular serving dish as follows. In the left-hand section, put one-third of the pasta mixed with a generous amount of hot tomato sauce – keep it warm on the stove until you need it. In the middle section, put another third mixed with the melted butter and lots of freshly grated Parmesan. In the right-hand section, put the last third of pasta mixed with the sautéed courgettes.

Tomato sauce Home-made tomato sauce is far tastier than store-bought versions. Use the recipe on page 37 and, if you like, substitute the tinned tomatoes with 500 g (1 lb 2 oz) peeled, deseeded and chopped fresh plum tomatoes. Follow the method as given, but simmer gently for 30 minutes.

LINGUINE CON LA PANCETTA
Linguine with pancetta & tomato sauce

There is no avoiding the Neapolitans' almost passionate culinary relationship with the tomato and, as this traditional Easter dish clearly and deliciously shows, why would you want to …

❖ SERVES 4

2 tablespoons olive oil
1 onion, finely chopped
100 g (3¹/2 oz) pancetta, diced
1 kg (2¹/4 lb) ripe tomatoes, peeled
   and chopped (see note on page 116)
2 or 3 large fresh basil leaves, plus
   extra, finely sliced, to garnish
400 g (14 oz) linguine
2 tablespoons freshly grated
   Parmesan cheese

Heat the oil in a pan over a medium heat, and sauté the onion and pancetta. Add the tomatoes and simmer over a low heat for 20 minutes. Tear the whole basil leaves into small pieces, sprinkle into the sauce and cook for a further 10 minutes.

Cook the linguine in a large pan of slightly salted boiling water until al dente. Drain and add to the sauce. Stir through, then sprinkle the extra basil and Parmesan over the top. Serve immediately.

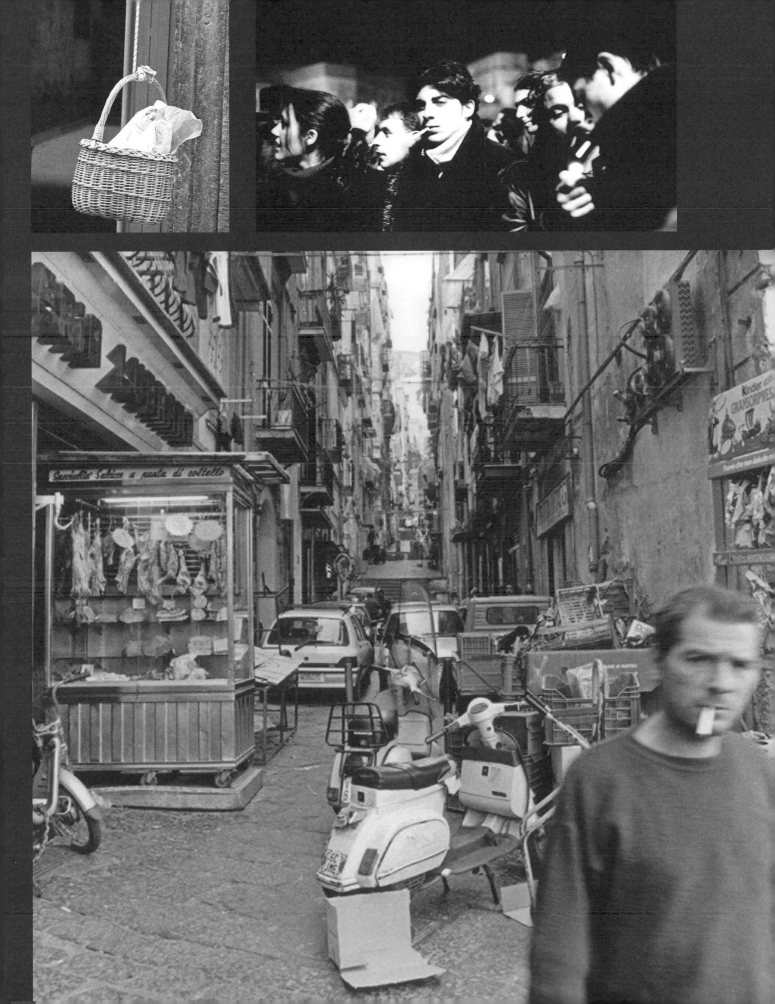

PENNETTE AL FORMAGGIO AL FORNO
Baked pennette with four cheeses

A *cucina povera* recipe, this pasta bake takes advantage of the array of cheeses produced in Campania, including the oddly named *caciocavallo* (horse's cheese).

✢ SERVES 4–6

500 g (1 lb 2 oz) pennette such as
  penne rigate
100 g (3¹/₂ oz) butter, plus extra for
  top of dish
150 g (5 oz) thickly sliced cooked
  ham, preferably Italian, diced
100 g (3¹/₂ oz) fontina cheese, diced
100 g (3¹/₂ oz) caciocavallo cheese,
  diced
200 g (7 oz) provola affumicata
  (smoked provolone cheese), diced
freshly grated Parmesan cheese
generous handful of coarse dried
  breadcrumbs (see note on page 19)
salt and freshly ground black pepper

Preheat the oven to 150°C (300°F/Gas 2). Cook the pennette in a large saucepan of slightly salted boiling water for 12 minutes until al dente.

While the pasta is cooking, melt the 100 g (3¹/₂ oz) butter in a pan over a medium heat and lightly brown the diced ham. Drain the pasta and add to the ham and butter. Add the fontina, caciocavallo and provola, mix well and transfer to a buttered baking dish. Sprinkle generously with grated Parmesan and top with the breadcrumbs. Dot with some extra butter and bake for 15 minutes. Serve immediately while the cheese is nice and stringy.

Caciocavallo cheese Similar to aged provolone, *caciocavallo* is made out of sheep's or cow's milk, has a hard edible rind and is shaped like a teardrop. The method for making it is believed to date from at least the fourteenth century and originated in Sicily. *Caciocavallo* literally means 'horse's cheese', a name that seems to have come from the way the cheese is left to dry by hanging two curds attached by string so that they straddle a horizontal pole or beam – *a cavallo*. Caciocavallo Silano (PDO) is a cow's milk version of the cheese that is made in designated areas of Campania, as well as in Basilicata, Calabria, Molise and Puglia.

LASAGNETTE CON LA RICOTTA
Fresh pasta bake with ricotta

Lasagnette is a narrower version of lasagne pasta. Like lasagne, its sheets can be wavy along one side or both, or straight along the edges. This pasta bake is often served during *Carnevale*, the traditional period of celebration before the advent of Lent.

✢ SERVES 4

200 g (7 oz) fresh ricotta
50 g (1³/₄ oz) butter, melted
50 g (1³/₄ oz) Parmesan cheese,
  grated, plus extra for sprinkling
pinch of freshly ground nutmeg
500 g (1 lb 2 oz) lasagnette
salt and freshly ground black pepper

Preheat the oven to 150°–160°C (300°–325°F/Gas 2–3). Mix the ricotta in a bowl with a little hot water, half of the melted butter, the Parmesan and a pinch of nutmeg. Season with salt and pepper. Set aside.

Cook the lasagnette in a large saucepan of slightly salted boiling water until al dente. Drain, then arrange a third of the pasta in a layer over the bottom of a large buttered ovenproof dish. Cover with a layer of the ricotta cream. Repeat the process, finishing off with a layer of pasta. Sprinkle with some extra grated Parmesan, pour over the remaining melted butter, and bake in the oven for about 30 minutes until the top is crispy and golden brown. Cut into slices and serve hot.

MACCHERONCELLI CON LE MELANZANE
Maccheroncelli with aubergine & cherry tomatoes

Cherry tomatoes and aubergines – and other vegetables and fruit – thrive in the region of rich volcanic soil around Mount Vesuvius, from where this recipes comes. They are used here to make a sauce for *maccheroncelli*, a long tube-shaped pasta slightly less than the thickness of a pencil.

⁘ SERVES 4

1 kg (2¹/₄ lb) aubergines
light olive oil for shallow-frying
600 g (1 lb 5 oz) maccheroncelli
  or similar long tube-shaped pasta
  such as bucatini or perciatelli
300 g (10 oz) cherry tomatoes, halved
about 2 tablespoons extra virgin olive
  oil for seasoning
1 tablespoon grated pecorino cheese
salt

Slice the aubergines and sprinkle with salt. Put in a colander and place a weight on top. Leave the aubergines to drain for 1 hour to draw out any bitter juices and the excess water. Rinse well under cold running water, shake the water off and pat the aubergines dry with a clean cloth or kitchen paper.

Heat enough oil for shallow-frying in a heavy pan over a medium-high heat. Shallow-fry the aubergines on both sides until crispy. Remove with a slotted spoon and drain on kitchen paper.

In the meantime, cook the pasta in a large pan of slightly salted boiling water until al dente. Drain. Add the aubergines, cherry tomatoes and extra virgin olive oil. Stir well, sprinkle with the pecorino and serve immediately.

PASTA E FAGIOLI
Pasta with cannellini beans

This is very much a country dish. In areas where meat was scarce or expensive, pulses were often used to provide necessary protein in the diet – and there was the added benefit that they were filling and could be used over the winter months when fresh produce was less available.

⁘ SERVES 4

300 g (10 oz) dried cannellini beans
pinch of bicarbonate of soda
2 tablespoons olive oil
2 garlic cloves, finely chopped
2 celery sticks, chopped
2 fresh tomatoes, peeled, deseeded
  and chopped (see page 116)
1 fresh red chilli, deseeded and
  finely chopped
2 tablespoons passata
300 g (10 oz) pasta mista
salt and freshly ground black pepper

Soak the beans overnight in plenty of cold water with a pinch of bicarbonate of soda. Rinse well, and put the beans in a pan with 1.5 litres (2³/₄ pints) water. Cover the pan and bring to the boil. Reduce the heat to low and simmer gently for 2 hours until the beans are tender but still have a bite.

In the meantime, make a tomato sauce. Heat the oil in a frying pan over a medium heat. Add the garlic, celery, tomatoes and chilli. Reduce the heat and simmer gently for 10 minutes until cooked down into a sauce.

When the beans are nearly cooked, add the tomato sauce and passata. Continue cooking for about 20 minutes. Remove some of the beans, blend until smooth and return to the pan.

Cook the pasta in plenty of slightly salted boiling water for half its cooking time. Add to the beans to finish cooking in the soup for a few minutes until al dente. Leave to stand for 5 minutes before serving.

RAGÙ DI CARNE
Classic slow-cooked meat & tomato sauce

A dish very much in the tradition of slow cooking, this rich *ragù* was originally created in the nineteenth century for Naples' noble families, a fact reflected in its use of meat and its more elaborate cooking method. It would certainly have been beyond the means of the city's poorer residents. Given the very long cooking time, it is a good idea to make the sauce the day before – the flavour only improves over time. The time and care devoted to preparing this dish led to its alternative name of *ragù, or sugo, della guardaporta* (doorkeeper's sauce), indicating the need for someone to watch over the pot while it cooked. It is actually two dishes in one: the meat is removed from the sauce and used as a main course, while the sauce is served with pasta.

✢ SERVES 4

1 kg (2¹/₄ lb) beef, silverside or pork fillets (ask your butcher for advice on the best cuts of beef)

3 sprigs of fresh flat-leaf parsley, leaves picked and finely chopped

50 g (1³/₄ oz) prosciutto crudo slices

2 tablespoons olive oil

50 g (1³/₄ oz) lard

300 g (10 oz) onions, chopped

1 or 2 garlic cloves, finely chopped

30 g (1 oz) bacon fat

60 g (2 oz) pancetta, chopped

1 litre (1³/₄ pints) dry red wine

300 g (10 oz) passata

salt and freshly ground black pepper

First prepare the meat rolls. Take the beef, silverside or pork fillets, and pound each one with a meat mallet or wooden rolling pin to flatten. (If you like, you can buy escalopes from your butcher already flattened and trimmed.) Cover each fillet with a sprinkling of parsley, then lay the prosciutto over the top. Season well with black pepper. Roll up and tie with butcher's string. Set aside.

Heat the oil and lard in a heavy saucepan over a medium heat, and sweat the onions, garlic, bacon fat and pancetta for a few minutes until the onion is soft and the pancetta is starting to brown. Add the meat rolls, cover the pan and cook over a gentle heat for about 5 minutes. When the onions start to turn golden brown, uncover the pan and add the red wine. Continue cooking over a gentle heat, stirring occasionally with a wooden spoon.

After a good hour, when all the liquid has reduced, add a little of the passata, stir, increase the heat slightly and cook until the sauce has turned a rich, dark colour. Add the rest of the passata, a little at a time. This process should take somewhere between 1¹/₂ and 2 hours. Add a couple of glasses of water, stir gently and increase the heat to medium. Cover the pan and simmer gently (known as *pippiare* in Italian) for a further 2 hours. When the meat is cooked through, remove from the sauce and transfer to a serving dish. Leave to rest in a warm place – this will provide your main course.

Continue simmering the *ragù* sauce until it is thick, dark and glossy. Meanwhile, cook your preferred pasta in a large saucepan of slightly salted boiling water until al dente. Drain and add to the sauce. Toss through and serve as a first course. The meat is served with roast potatoes or a mixed green salad, or another vegetable side dish.

TUBETTI CON LE FAVE
Tubetti with fresh broad beans

Fresh broad beans are just one of the many vegetable crops with an important place in Campania's cuisine. At the beginning of the season, when they are at their most tender, they are often slipped out of their skins and eaten raw, dressed with seasoned olive oil. Later in the season they appear in stews and soups. Here, in this dish from the region around Mount Vesuvius, renowned for the choice broad beans grown in its volcanic soil, the beans are first sweated gently, then cooked with the pasta, to produce a flavourful lunch or supper dish.

⊹ SERVES 4

2 tablespoons olive oil
1 bunch of spring onions,
  finely chopped
75 g (2¹/₂ oz) pancetta or speck, diced
250 g (9 oz) shelled fresh tender
  broad beans
300 g (10 oz) tubetti rigati or similar
  large tube-shaped pasta such as
  ditali or pennette
handful of fresh flat-leaf parsley,
  leaves picked and chopped, to serve
salt and freshly ground black pepper
freshly grated pecorino cheese,
  to serve

Heat the olive oil in a large saucepan over a medium heat, and gently sweat the spring onions, pancetta or speck, and broad beans for a few minutes. Season well with salt and black pepper, and cook for 10–15 minutes until the beans are just tender (it is important not to let them become mushy). Add enough water to the pan to cook the pasta. When it comes to a rolling boil, add the tubetti and cook until al dente. Drain, transfer to a serving dish and sprinkle generously with the chopped parsley and plenty of freshly grated pecorino. Serve immediately.

LINGUINE CON FUNGHI E GAMBERONI
Linguine with mushrooms & king prawns

Mushrooms and king prawns combine perfectly in this simple but classic pasta dish, which is ideal for a quick supper or lunch. The recipe hails from the resort town of Castellammare di Stabia, situated on Campania's Sorrento Peninsula south of Naples and famed for its mineral springs.

✤ SERVES 4

2 tablespoons olive oil

2 garlic cloves, finely chopped

8–12 fresh raw king prawns, peeled
  and deveined

200 g (7 oz) button mushrooms,
  finely sliced

100 g (3¹/₂ oz) Italian cooked ham,
  finely sliced

1 glass of Cognac

2 glasses of dry white wine

100 ml (3¹/₂ fl oz) good-quality
  vegetable stock

about 125 ml (4 fl oz) double cream

400 g (14 oz) linguine

salt and freshly ground black pepper

generous handful of fresh flat-leaf
  parsley, chopped, to serve

Heat the oil in a large pan over a medium-high heat, and sweat the garlic for a couple of minutes until starting to soften. Add the prawns and season with salt and black pepper, sauté for a minute or so, then tip in the mushrooms and ham. Pour over the Cognac and allow it to reduce completely. Repeat the process with the white wine, until it has reduced as well. Next, pour in the stock and reduce the heat to medium. Continue cooking for a further 10 minutes before adding the cream.

Meanwhile, cook the pasta in a large saucepan of slightly salted boiling water until al dente. Drain, adding to the prawn and mushroom sauce after you have added the cream. Increase the heat slightly, and quickly stir through to mix everything together well. Serve hot, with a good sprinkling of chopped parsley over the top.

CONCHIGLIE CON OLIO E LIMONE
Conchiglie with oil & lemon

Ideal on a hot summer's day, this cold pasta dish relies on using top-quality ingredients – pasta made from durum wheat, the finest extra virgin olive oil and fragrant, juicy lemons. Lemons thrive in Campania's climate, and those from Sorrento, Capri and Procida are particularly prized.

✣ SERVES 4

400 g (14 oz) conchiglie
   (dried pasta shells)
extra virgin olive oil for drizzling
juice of 1 lemon
3 spring onions, green parts only,
   finely sliced on the diagonal
3 sprigs of fresh flat-leaf parsley,
   leaves picked and finely chopped
salt and freshly ground black pepper

Cook the pasta in a large saucepan of slightly salted boiling water until al dente. Drain well. Place in a serving dish, drizzle with extra virgin olive oil, stir thoroughly and leave to cool. When the pasta is quite cold, pour over a little more olive oil, and season with salt and black pepper. Squeeze over the lemon juice, and sprinkle with the spring onions and finely chopped parsley.

PASTA E ZUCCA
Pasta with pumpkin

The area surrounding Mount Vesuvius, with its fertile volcanic soil, produces lots of high-quality vegetables, and many recipes from the region make the most of what grows so well and so abundantly. Choose a good variety of pumpkin for this dish, one with firm orange flesh and not too watery, to bring out the contrast between the creamy sweetness and the hint of chilli.

✣ SERVES 4

olive oil
3 garlic cloves, finely chopped
1 kg (2¼ lb) pumpkin or butternut
   squash, peeled, seeds removed and
   cut into dice
pinch of freshly grated nutmeg
1 fresh red chilli, deseeded and
   finely chopped
500 g (1 lb 2 oz) tubetti
generous handful of fresh flat-leaf
   parsley, leaves picked and chopped
salt and freshly ground black pepper

Heat a generous amount of oil in a pan over a medium heat. Add the garlic and sweat for a few minutes until soft and starting to caramelize. Add the diced pumpkin, nutmeg and chilli. Season with salt and black pepper. Pour in a little water, and cook over a gentle heat for at least 15 minutes until the pumpkin breaks down into a thick, smooth sauce.

Cook the pasta in a large pan of slightly salted boiling water until al dente. Drain, reserving a little of the cooking water. Add the pasta to the pumpkin sauce with a sprinkling of chopped parsley. Stir through. If the sauce is too dry, add a little of the reserved cooking water from the pasta to thin it slightly.

VERMICELLI AGLIO E OLIO
Vermicelli with garlic & oil

Simple but delicious – everything that embodies a dish from the *cucina povera* heritage. It is also very quick to make and requires only ingredients that you will almost always have on hand.

✣ SERVES 4

600 g (1 lb 5 oz) vermicelli
200 ml (7 fl oz) olive oil
4 garlic cloves, finely chopped
3 fresh red chillies, deseeded and
  finely chopped
handful of fresh flat-leaf parsley,
  leaves picked and chopped
salt and freshly ground black pepper

Cook the pasta in a large saucepan of slightly salted boiling water until al dente. While the pasta is cooking, heat the oil in a frying pan over a medium heat, and sweat the garlic and chilli (you do not want the garlic to brown and become bitter). When the garlic is soft and starting to caramelize, remove from the heat and add the parsley. Drain the pasta, transfer to a serving dish and pour over the garlic oil. Stir through well and serve immediately.

INSALATA DI RISO
Rice salad with tuna, eggs & fontina

Readily meeting the *cucina povera* requirements of being filling and tasty, this rice salad is perfect for an al fresco lunch or even a picnic. It is worth buying tuna preserved in oil in a jar rather than a tin if you can, as the taste is far superior. Look for it in delicatessens and gourmet food shops.

✣ SERVES 4

500 g (1 lb 2 oz) long-grain rice
4 tablespoons extra virgin olive oil,
  plus extra for drizzling
4 ripe salad tomatoes
2 tablespoons freshly squeezed
  lemon juice
2 or 3 large fresh basil leaves,
  finely sliced
1 x 200-g (7-oz) jar tuna in oil,
  drained and broken up into flakes
50 g (1³/₄ oz) green olives, pitted
  and halved
100 g (3¹/₂ oz) fontina cheese, diced
3 hard-boiled eggs, diced
salt and freshly ground black pepper

Cook the rice, drizzle with 2 tablespoons of the extra virgin olive oil, stir well and leave to cool.

Chop the tomatoes, drizzle with a little oil and season with salt. Allow to sit for 5 minutes. Make a vinaigrette with 2 tablespoons of the extra virgin olive oil, lemon juice and basil, and pour over the rice. Add all the other ingredients and mix well. Leave to rest in the refrigerator for 30 minutes or so, and serve chilled.

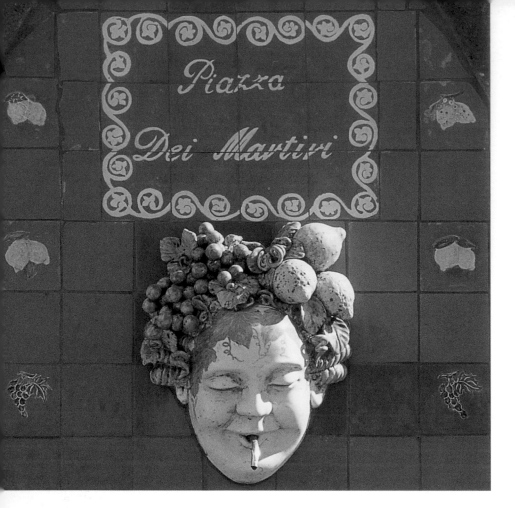

RISO BELLA NAPOLI
Creamy rice with fresh tomato & basil sauce

The tomato is so highly regarded in Campania that it should come as no surprise that it features in this Neapolitan version of risotto, which has its roots in the convent tradition. Unlike a risotto, the tomato sauce is made separately and stirred through once the rice is cooked.

✤ SERVES 4

100 g (3¹/₂ oz) pancetta, diced
2 tablespoons olive oil
1 onion, finely chopped
600 g (1 lb 5 oz) ripe tomatoes,
  peeled and chopped (see page 116)
4 or 5 large fresh basil leaves, torn
1 litre (1³/₄ pints) hot good-quality
  vegetable stock
60 g (2 oz) butter
400 g (14 oz) arborio or carnaroli rice
60 g (2 oz) Parmesan cheese, grated
salt and freshly ground black pepper

Sweat the pancetta in the oil with half the onion over a medium heat until the onion is soft and starting to caramelize. Add the tomatoes and basil, and season with salt and black pepper. Simmer gently for 30 minutes.

In the meantime, keep the stock hot in a saucepan for adding to the rice. Heat the butter in another saucepan and sweat the remaining onion until soft and starting to caramelize. Pour in a little of the stock while the onions are cooking. When the onions have reduced, add the rice, stir for a few minutes until the rice is coated in the butter, then pour in half the stock. Add the rest of the stock to the rice a little at a time, stirring continuously with a wooden spoon. Cook for about 20 minutes, stirring, until the rice is cooked but still has a slight bite, and nearly all the stock has been absorbed. Add the tomato sauce and Parmesan cheese. Stir through to mix thoroughly, and leave to stand for a few minutes before serving.

SECONDI PIATTI
Main courses

PETTO DI POLLO AROMATICO
Spicy chicken roulades in tomato sauce

There is little meat in much of Campania's regional cuisine. What there is usually comes from the two other historical elements that have had such a profound influence on the area's food: the royal and noble households of the French and Spanish courts, and the monasteries and convents. This recipe originates from the convents, and bears that unmistakable Campanian touch in its use of fresh herbs and a rich tomato sauce.

✛ SERVES 4

500 g (1 lb 2 oz) chicken breast fillet
2 or 3 stalks of fresh flat-leaf parsley,
  leaves picked and roughly chopped
1–2 garlic cloves, finely chopped
4 tablespoons freshly grated
  pecorino cheese
4 tablespoons freshly grated
  Parmesan cheese
small handful of fresh mint leaves,
  roughly chopped
2 whole fresh bay leaves,
  roughly chopped
sprig of fresh rosemary, leaves picked
  and chopped
1 fresh sage leaf, roughly chopped
2 tablespoons olive oil for cooking
1 glass of dry white wine
500 g (1 lb 2 oz) passata
1 fresh red chilli, deseeded and
  finely chopped
salt and freshly ground black pepper
small handful of large fresh basil
  leaves, rolled and finely sliced into
  chiffonade, to serve

To make the chicken roulades, slice each breast fillet through the middle so that you are left with 2 thinner fillets. If you find it easier, or the fillets are not big enough, pound out the chicken using a meat mallet or wooden rolling pin, then cut each fillet in half lengthways. Trim the edges to neaten, if necessary. Lay out the slices of breast fillet side by side on a work surface. Put a little parsley on each slice, reserving some for later use, then divide up the garlic, pecorino and Parmesan, and use to cover each slice. Season with salt and black pepper. Roll up the chicken into roulades, starting from one of the short edges, and secure with toothpicks or cocktail sticks.

Add the remaining parsley, the mint, bay leaves, rosemary and sage to a heavy pan over a medium heat with the oil. Quickly brown the roulades on all sides. When they are nicely browned, pour over the white wine and continue cooking for 20 minutes until the wine has reduced, turning the roulades from time to time. Add the passata, sprinkle in the chilli and season with salt. Cover the pan and leave to simmer over a gentle heat for 20 minutes. When the roulades are cooked, sprinkle with the basil and serve immediately, accompanied by a fresh green salad or a vegetable side dish such as lightly sautéed courgettes.

TORTINO NAPOLETANO
Meatloaf with courgette & mashed potato

The courgettes used in this traditional convent recipe keep the meatloaf moist and soften the texture, while the smoked provolone melts into the meat beneath the fluffy potato topping.

✣ SERVES 4

50 g (1³/4 oz) butter plus extra for
  mashing and topping
2-3 tablespoons olive oil
2 onions, finely sliced
1 kg (2¹/4 lb) lean beef mince
1 kg (2¹/4 lb) floury potatoes
1 kg (2¹/4 lb) courgettes, sliced
  into rounds
1 garlic clove, finely chopped
a few fresh basil leaves, chopped
handful of dried breadcrumbs (see
  note on page 19)
150 g (5 oz) provola affumicata
  (smoked provolone cheese), diced
salt and freshly ground black pepper

Preheat the oven to 160°C (325°F/Gas 3). Heat the butter and oil in a heavy pan over a medium heat, and sweat the onions for a few minutes until soft and starting to caramelize. Add the meat and brown, stirring frequently and using a wooden spoon to break up the meat. When the meat is nicely browned, remove from the heat and set aside.

Boil the potatoes with their skins on, peel and mash. Add a little butter and salt. Using a clean pan, sauté the courgettes and garlic in a little oil over a medium heat for a few minutes until just starting to colour. Stir in the basil, then add the courgettes to the meat and stir through. Season with salt and black pepper.

Transfer the mixture to a buttered ovenproof dish and sprinkle with the breadcrumbs. Scatter over the diced provolone, cover with the mashed potato and dot with extra butter. Bake in the oven for 45 minutes. If the topping is starting to brown too much, cover the dish with foil – this will also help to keep the meatloaf moist. Cut into slices and serve.

FETTINE ALLA PIZZAIOLA
Slices of beef with tomato & oregano

Pizzaiola is a traditional Neapolitan tomato sauce seasoned with oregano that can also be used with pasta such as spaghetti or maccheroncelli. Here it is used to cover slices of beef, which are gently slow-cooked in the *pizzaiola* sauce to produce a meltingly tender, flavourful main course.

✣ SERVES 4

2 tablespoons olive oil
3 garlic cloves, finely chopped
1 kg (2¹/4 lb) beef or veal escalopes or
  thin, tender steaks such as sirloin
500 g (1 lb 2 oz) ripe tomatoes,
  peeled, deseeded and chopped
  (see page 116)
1 tablespoon dried oregano
salt and freshly ground black pepper

Heat the oil in a large heavy pan over a medium heat, and sweat the garlic for a few minutes until soft and translucent. Add the beef or veal, and cook for 15 minutes until browned on both sides. Add the tomatoes and season with salt and black pepper. Crush the oregano lightly in the palm of your hand, then sprinkle over the top. Simmer over a gentle heat for 45 minutes until the meat is very tender and the sauce has reduced and thickened. Serve the beef slices topped with the *pizzaiola* sauce.

CAPRETTO UOVA E FORMAGGIO
Braised kid with eggs & cheese

Kid meat is called *capretto* in Italy, and is far more tender than mature goat meat. Choose the tenderest cuts for this traditional Easter dish, preferably leg or loin, or even some parts of the shoulder or breast. If you cannot find kid, substitute with tender boned lamb.

✢ SERVES 4

1.5 kg (3 lb 3 oz) boned kid such as
  leg or loin
plain flour for coating
2 tablespoons olive oil
2 garlic cloves, finely chopped
1 onion, finely chopped
500 g (1 lb 2 oz) freshly shelled
  green peas
4 large eggs
pinch of salt
2 tablespoons freshly grated
  Parmesan cheese
juice of 1 lemon
salt and freshly ground black pepper

Clean the meat well, rinse and pat dry with kitchen paper. Cut into large cubes, and coat lightly in the flour. Heat the oil in a large heavy pan over a medium heat, and sweat the onion and garlic until soft and starting to caramelize. Remove a little of the onion mixture and set aside in a small pan for cooking the peas. Add the kid to the large pan, and sauté for a few minutes until the meat is browned all over. Season with salt and black pepper. Add just enough water to keep the meat moist, and cook very slowly over a gentle heat for about 1 hour until the meat is tender. Keep adding a little water as necessary, so that the meat does not dry out.

About 15 minutes before the end of the cooking time, reheat the reserved onion mixture over a gentle heat. Add the peas and sweat for a few minutes, then tip the contents of the pan into the meat. When the meat is ready, beat the eggs with a pinch of salt and the Parmesan. Pour into the pan and cook, stirring all the time, until all the meat is well coated (in a similar way to making spaghetti carbonara). Turn off the heat, quickly pour over the lemon juice and stir through. Remove from the heat and serve immediately.

SPEZZATINO CON I PISELLI
Beef stew with peas & rosemary

Slow-cooking to bring flavour to the fore is a fundamental aspect of a number of traditional dishes in Campanian cuisine, such as this beef stew which came out of the convent kitchens.

✢ SERVES 4

30 g (1 oz) butter
2 tablespoons olive oil
1 onion, roughly chopped
1 kg (2¹/₄ lb) stewing beef, cubed
1 kg (2¹/₄ lb) freshly shelled green
  peas
1 litre (1³/₄ pints) beef stock
100 g (3¹/₂ oz) passata
a few sprigs of fresh rosemary, leaves
  picked and chopped
salt and freshly ground black pepper

Heat the butter and oil in a heavy pan over a medium heat, and sweat the onion for a few minutes until soft and starting to caramelize. Add the meat and cook for 10 minutes until browned on all sides. Add the peas and continue cooking for a few minutes more.

Pour in the stock and passata, sprinkle in the rosemary, and season with salt and black pepper. Simmer very gently over a medium heat, uncovered, for about 1 hour until the sauce has reduced and the meat is tender. Serve hot with mashed or roast potatoes.

REGIONAL WINE-MAKING

After years of stagnation, Campanian wine production is now enjoying increasing success around the world. This is due to the introduction of new policies and to controls which balance the ever-increasing need for technological innovation with traditional methods. An increase in cellar facilities and new vineyard plantings are two direct results of this, as well as the adoption of more modern vinification techniques.

However, the region's wine-makers have not only looked to the new in order to revitalize the industry and raise standards. Many plantings and re-plantings have actually been of old grape types that are particular to the region, drawing on Campania's highly distinctive wine heritage. Ancient vines such as Vitis Hellenica, Vitis Apiana and Vitis Aminea Gemina, as well as 'timeless' wines such as Falerno, Faustiniano and Caleno, are all individual enough to withstand the anonymous effects of the globalization of the wine market. In Campania, each wine is seen as a direct expression of the land, derived from both its geographical and historical characteristics. Wine is seen as a cultural ambassador – a banner where the terrain and the proverbial hospitality of its land of origin are inscribed.

Notable wineries, both large estates and family-owned businesses, include the relatively new Feudi di San Gregorio (producers of Taurasi and Greco di Tufo, among others), as well as Caggiano, Caputo, Maffini, Marisa Cuomo, Benito Ferraro, Mastroberardino, Mustilli, Villa Matilde and Vestini Campagnano. If Feudi di San Gregorio can be seen as the new face of Campanian viticulture and wine-making, Mastroberardino perhaps represents both the traditional and the modern.

The Mastroberardino family has been making wine for more than 300 years. Committed to improving Campania's wine industry, the family firmly believes in taking advantage of new vinification techniques, whilst maintaining the history and cultural identity of Campanian wine. Mastroberardino has been responsible for much of the revival of Pompeiian vineyards, growing grape varieties such as Fiano, Greco di Tufo and Aglianico, and produces very good Taurasi. Similar family-owned ventures such as Villa Matilde, responsible for much of the Falerno grape's rejuvenation, and Mustilli, which grows Greco, Falanghina, Piedirosso and Aglianico, also carry the torch for Campanian wine tradition.

BRACIOLONE ALLA NAPOLETANA
Pork roulade with prosciutto, Parmesan & parsley

In Campania and elsewhere in Southern Italy, the term *braciola* refers to a slice of meat such as veal rolled up around a filling; in other parts of Italy this is usually known as *involtini*. A *braciolone* is simply a large *braciola*, where several slices of meat are rolled together to form a roulade, as seen in this classic Neapolitan recipe for pork.

✢ SERVES 4–6

1.25 kg (2³/4 lb) pork fillet or
  boned shoulder of pork
200 g (7 oz) lean pork mince
150 g (5 oz) prosciutto or pancetta,
  chopped
30 g (1 oz) Parmesan cheese, grated
50 g (1³/4 oz) sultanas
50 g (1³/4 oz) pine nuts
1 hard-boiled egg, chopped
1 garlic clove, finely chopped
handful of fresh flat-leaf parsley,
  leaves picked and chopped
50 g (1³/4 oz) dried breadcrumbs
  (see note on page 19)
1 tablespoon olive oil
50 g (1³/4 oz) lard
1 onion, cut into fine wedges
500 ml (16 fl oz) red wine
500 g (1 lb 2 oz) ripe tomatoes,
  peeled, deseeded and diced
  (see note on page 116)
pinch of sugar (optional)
salt and freshly ground black pepper

Cut the meat into thin slices lengthways. (Alternatively, you can slit the pork lengthways down the middle, about halfway through.) Using a smooth meat mallet or wooden rolling pin, pound the meat to flatten slightly if necessary. Trim away any rough edges to neaten. On a flat work surface, arrange the pieces in a row one next to the other, slightly overlapping the edges. Make a stuffing using the mince, prosciutto or pancetta, Parmesan, sultanas, pine nuts, hard-boiled egg, garlic, parsley and breadcrumbs. Season with salt and black pepper. Combine all the ingredients thoroughly, and spread the stuffing over the meat. Roll the meat up firmly like a Swiss roll, and tie in place with butcher's string, securing in enough places along the length of the roulade to keep the meat in a tight roll and the stuffing in place. Also tie at each end like a sausage so that the stuffing doesn't ooze out.

Heat the oil and lard in a deep-sided heavy frying pan over a medium heat. Brown the roulade on all sides with the onion – you want the meat to colour before it starts cooking in the sauce. Pour over the red wine and allow to reduce for 10 minutes. Add the tomatoes, cover the pan and cook for about an hour, turning the meat from time to time. Towards the end of the cooking time, season the sauce with salt and black pepper, and if necessary a little sugar to cut the tartness of the tomatoes. Cut the pork into thick slices and serve with green beans and roast potatoes, or other vegetable side dishes.

SALSICCE DEL PRETE
Pan-fried sausages with new potatoes & chilli

As the literal name of this recipe – priest's sausages – suggests, this is another dish to emerge from the monasteries and convents of Campania.

✢ SERVES 4

2 tablespoons lard or olive oil
500 g (1 lb 2 oz) new potatoes,
  unpeeled and sliced
1 fresh red chilli, deseeded and
  finely chopped
1 kg (2¹/₄ lb) fresh Italian pork
  sausages
salt and freshly ground black pepper

Heat half the lard or oil in a frying pan over a medium heat. Add the potatoes and sauté for 20 minutes. Meanwhile, in a separate pan, heat the remaining lard or oil. Add the chilli and a good grinding of black pepper and finally the sausages. Fry for about 15 minutes until the sausages are well browned. Once the potatoes are cooked, tip into the same pan as the sausages. Stir through gently and serve immediately.

SALSICCE AL CARTOCCIO
Charcoal-grilled sausages in a parcel

In culinary terms, *al cartoccio* means to cook something in a wrapper – in this case foil-wrapped sausages which are grilled in the hot charcoal of a barbecue. This cooking method imparts an intriguing smoky element to the flavourful herby sausages used in this traditional dish from the Campanian countryside.

✢ SERVES 4

1 tablespoon lard or olive oil
1 kg (2¹/₄ lb) fresh Italian fennel
  sausages or similar

Heat a charcoal barbecue or grill until the charcoal is white-hot. Take some pieces of foil and grease with the lard or oil. Arrange the sausages in twos on each piece of foil and wrap tightly. Carefully place in the hot charcoal ashes and leave the sausages to grill for about 30 minutes, making sure that they do not burn or become charred. Remove from the charcoal using a pair of tongs, carefully unwrap the foil and serve the sausages hot, with the vegetable side dishes of your choice as an accompaniment.

SALSICCE ALLA CONTADINA
Country-style sausages with lentils

Another traditional dish from the countryside surrounding Naples, this one includes lentils. Pulses are an important staple in much of the regional cuisine, particularly in those dishes that fall into the category of *cucina povera*. They were a much-needed source of protein in a diet where meat was both scarce and expensive.

✣ SERVES 4

2 garlic cloves

400 g (14 oz) brown lentils such as Puy, picked and rinsed

2 tablespoons olive oil

1 carrot, roughly chopped

1 celery stick, roughly chopped

1 kg (2¼ lb) fresh Italian pork sausages

400 g (14 oz) ripe tomatoes, peeled, deseeded and chopped (see note on page 116)

salt and freshly ground black pepper

Roughly chop 1 clove of the garlic. Put in a pan with the lentils, cover with water and bring to the boil over a medium heat. Simmer for 20 minutes, then remove from the heat but do not drain.

In the meantime, finely chop the remaining clove of garlic. Heat the oil in a heavy frying pan over a medium heat. Sweat the chopped garlic, carrot and celery for a few minutes until soft. Add the sausages and brown in the pan, then add the tomatoes. Continue cooking for about 15 minutes until the tomatoes have broken down and the sauce has thickened. Add the lentils with their cooking liquid, and season with salt and black pepper. Simmer gently for a further 15 minutes. Serve hot.

CONIGLIO ALLA NONNA RITA
Braised rabbit with onions & brandy

Ischia Porto is one of two distinct districts that make up Ischia, the major town on the volcanic island of the same name. It grew up around the island's main harbour, and the dockside restaurants and bars readily attract the streams of visitors travelling to and fro. This recipe was created for Ischia Porto's Nonna Rita restaurant.

✛ SERVES 4

2 tablespoons olive oil
1 rabbit, about 1 kg (2¼ lb)
2 garlic cloves, finely chopped
1 fresh red chilli, deseeded and
  finely chopped
1 glass of brandy or white wine
1 kg (2¼ lb) onions, sliced
2 or 3 ripe tomatoes, peeled,
  deseeded and chopped
1 whole bay leaf (fresh if possible)
2 or 3 sprigs of fresh rosemary,
  leaves picked
salt

Clean the rabbit and cut into pieces, making sure that you remove the gland at the bottom of the spine. Heat the oil in a heavy frying pan over a medium heat, and sauté the rabbit pieces for 10 minutes until nicely browned, cooking in batches if necessary. Return all the rabbit to the pan, and add the garlic and chilli. Sweat for a few minutes until soft and starting to caramelize.

Pour in the brandy or wine, and allow to reduce for 5 minutes. Add the onions, tomatoes, bay leaf and rosemary. Season with salt. Add a little water if necessary – just enough to keep the sauce moist. Cover the pan and cook for about an hour, stirring occasionally and keeping an eye on the sauce to make sure it doesn't dry out (add more water as necessary). Slow-cooking rabbit in this way helps to keep it tender and moist. Serve hot with roast potatoes or other vegetable side dishes. You could also use the sauce to serve with pasta such as penne or vermicelli.

CONIGLIO ALL'ISCHITANA
Braised rabbit with wine, tomato & herbs

Rabbit is a speciality on Ischia, so much so that old and long-revered techniques for breeding are still practised by the island's farmers. The rabbits are raised in ditches until they are fully grown, to produce the best possible meat. The recipe here is a traditional one.

✛ SERVES 4

1 rabbit, about 1 kg (2¼ lb)
2 tablespoons olive oil
sprig of fresh rosemary, leaves picked
about 2 glasses of dry white wine
500 g (1 lb 2 oz) ripe tomatoes,
  peeled, deseeded and chopped
2 or 3 large fresh basil leaves,
  chopped
salt and freshly ground black pepper

Clean the rabbit and cut into pieces, making sure that you remove the gland at the bottom of the spine. Heat the oil in a heavy pan over a medium heat. Add the rabbit and rosemary, and sauté for 10 minutes until the rabbit is nicely browned all over. Pour over the white wine and leave to reduce completely, before adding the tomato and basil. Season with salt and black pepper, and stir through.

Cover the pan and braise the rabbit for about 1 hour, stirring occasionally and adding a little more wine and just enough water to keep the rabbit moist. After an hour, increase the heat for a few minutes, turning the rabbit pieces to give them an even flavour. Serve immediately.

SCALOPPINE DI MONTAGNA
Veal escalopes with prosciutto, capers & mushrooms

Gutsy flavours and hearty ingredients are trademarks of dishes from the mountain regions of Campania, reflecting the strength of the people who made their lives in this rugged environment.

✢ SERVES 4

1 kg (2¹/₄ lb) veal escalopes
plain flour for dredging
100 g (3¹/₂ oz) prosciutto crudo slices
500 g (1 lb 2 oz) ripe tomatoes, sliced
3–4 teaspoons salted capers, rinsed
 and gently squeezed dry
150 g (5 oz) Italian mushrooms in oil
2 tablespoons chopped fresh oregano
2 tablespoons chopped fresh
 flat-leaf parsley
2 tablespoons chopped fresh basil
olive oil for drizzling
salt and freshly ground black pepper

Preheat the oven to 160°C (325°F/Gas 3). If the veal is not already flattened, use a smooth meat mallet or wooden rolling pin to pound the veal lightly to an even thickness. Heat a lightly oiled ridged grill pan or griddle over a medium-high heat. Dredge the veal in the flour, shaking off any excess. Quickly sear the veal in the pan for a couple of minutes on both sides.

Transfer to an oiled baking dish, arranging the pieces of veal side by side. Place slices of prosciutto, slices of tomato, some capers and mushrooms on each one. Season with salt and a little pepper. Sprinkle over the oregano, parsley and basil, and drizzle with oil. Cover the dish with foil, and bake in the oven for 15–20 minutes, removing the foil halfway through cooking. Serve immediately.

LE FETTINE DI PULCINELLA
Veal in white wine with cherry tomatoes & mushrooms

Pulcinella, a popular figure in Neapolitan puppetry, gives his name to this *cucina povera* dish.

✢ SERVES 4

500 g (1 lb 2 oz) veal escalopes
plain flour for dredging
a little olive oil
2 glasses of dry white wine
300 g (10 oz) cherry tomatoes
100 g (3¹/₂ oz) Italian cooked ham,
 chopped
300 g (3¹/₂ oz) button mushrooms,
 sliced
salt and freshly ground black pepper
handful of fresh flat-leaf parsley,
 chopped, to garnish

If the veal is not already flattened, use a smooth meat mallet or wooden rolling pin to pound the veal lightly to an even thickness. Dredge the veal in the flour, shaking off any excess. Heat a little olive oil in a large heavy pan over a medium heat, add the veal and brown for a minute or two on each side. Add the white wine and allow to reduce for 10 minutes.

Gently crush the cherry tomatoes, and add to the pan with the ham and mushrooms. Season with salt and black pepper, and allow to cook gently for 30 minutes. Sprinkle with chopped parsley and serve immediately.

POLPETTE ALLA NAPOLETANA
Meatballs in tomato sauce

Polpette (meatballs) and *polpettone* (meatloaf) feature throughout Italian cuisine. In this version from Campania's convent tradition, naturally enough the juicy meatballs are cooked in a rich tomato sauce. The meatloaf below is also a convent recipe, and has a scamorza cheese filling. Scamorza is made from cow's milk and is similar in many ways to mozzarella. It melts far better when baked, however, and its smoked version adds a lovely depth of flavour.

✣ SERVES 4

500 g (1 lb 2 oz) stale crustless bread
  such as ciabatta or pane casereccio
a little milk
500 g (1 lb 2 oz) lean beef mince
handful of fresh flat-leaf parsley,
  leaves picked and chopped
1 garlic clove, finely chopped
1 large egg, lightly beaten
50 g (1¾ oz) freshly grated
  Parmesan cheese
45 g (1½ oz) sultanas (optional)
45 g (1½ oz) pine nuts (optional)
light olive oil for cooking
1 small onion, finely chopped
600 g (1 lb 5 oz) tinned whole peeled
  plum tomatoes
salt and freshly ground black pepper

Soak the bread in a little milk. Squeeze gently to remove any excess liquid and place in a bowl with the mince, parsley and garlic. Mix well and add the egg, a pinch of salt, black pepper, Parmesan, sultanas and pine nuts (if using). Combine thoroughly with your hands. Shape into meatballs, and fry in plenty of hot oil in a large heavy pan over a medium heat for 10 minutes. Keep turning the meatballs carefully to prevent them catching on the bottom of the pan. Remove from the pan, drain on kitchen paper and set aside.

Meanwhile, make the tomato sauce. Sweat the onion in a little olive oil in a heavy pan over a medium heat until soft and translucent. Add the tomatoes and season with salt and black pepper. Transfer the meatballs to the sauce and cook for 10 minutes to heat through. Serve hot.

Polpettone – meatloaf with prosciutto, scamorza and Parmesan
Preheat the oven to 180°C (350°F/Gas 4). Soak 500 g (1 lb 2 oz) bread in 1 litre (1¾ pints) milk, drain and squeeze the bread gently to remove any excess liquid. Put in a bowl with 500 g (1 lb 2 oz) lean beef or pork mince, 2 eggs, 1 finely chopped garlic clove, 1 tablespoon freshly grated Parmesan cheese and a handful of chopped fresh flat-leaf parsley leaves. Season well with salt and freshly ground black pepper. Combine thoroughly with your hands, and pat out into a rectangle about 2 cm (1 in) thick.

Cut 100 g (3½ oz) prosciutto and 60 g (2 oz) smoked scamorza cheese into thin strips, and arrange over the mince mixture. Put 2 whole hard-boiled eggs on top, and wrap the meat around the eggs, shaping it into a meatloaf. (This is easier if your hands are wet.) Carefully transfer to an oiled baking dish – you need one larger than the meatloaf, so that you will be able to turn the loaf during cooking. Bake in the preheated oven for 40 minutes, turning from time to time. Cut into slices and serve hot.

INSALATA DI CARNE
Rocket salad with warm grilled beef, cherry tomatoes & basil

A perfect dish for al fresco dining, this salad works beautifully as part of a selection of dishes for a lunch for family or friends. It is a classic summertime dish that is very popular in Naples. Choose the ripest, sweetest cherry tomatoes you can find.

✢ SERVES 4–6

1 kg (2¼ lb) beef fillet or similar
   tender cut of beef
olive oil for grilling
100 g (3½ oz) young rocket leaves
   (if you use larger rocket leaves, tear
   before using)
500 g (1 lb 2 oz) ripe cherry
   tomatoes, halved
a few fresh basil leaves, chopped
2 garlic cloves, finely chopped
a little extra virgin olive oil
salt and freshly ground black pepper

Rub the beef fillet all over with olive oil, and season well on all sides with salt and black pepper. Heat a ridged grill pan or heavy frying pan over a medium-high heat and add the beef. Grill for 20–25 minutes, turning occasionally to brown all over, until the beef is well cooked (if you prefer your meat to be a little pink in the middle, simply cook for slightly less time). Leave to rest for a few minutes.

Meanwhile, put the rocket, tomatoes, basil and garlic in a large bowl. Season with salt and black pepper, and drizzle with a little extra virgin olive oil. Once the meat has rested, cut into slices and arrange on a serving platter. Arrange the salad over the top, and serve immediately.

BACCALÀ IN PASTELLA
Battered salt cod fillets

Baccalà, or salt cod, is popular across much of the Mediterranean, in Portugal, Spain and Italy. Naples is no exception, where it was embraced as part of *cucina povera* because it was cheap, readily available and kept for such a long time.

✢ SERVES 4

250 g (9 oz) plain flour
25 g (scant 1 oz) fresh yeast
pinch of salt
60 ml (2 fl oz) hot water
600 g (1 lb 5 oz) salt cod, soaked in
   several changes of cold water for
   24 hours
vegetable oil for deep-frying
salt and freshly ground black pepper

Make a batter with the flour, yeast, a pinch of salt and the hot water. Mix vigorously, cover and leave to rise for 30 minutes in a warm, dry place.

In the meantime, rinse the salt cod and remove the bones and skin. Put in a saucepan, with plenty of water and bring to the boil. Reduce the heat and simmer for about 10 minutes. Drain well, then break up the salt cod into flakes and add to the batter.

Heat enough oil for deep-frying in a high-sided heavy pan until very hot. Drop in spoonfuls of the salt cod batter. Serve the fritters piping hot with a sprinkling of salt and black pepper.

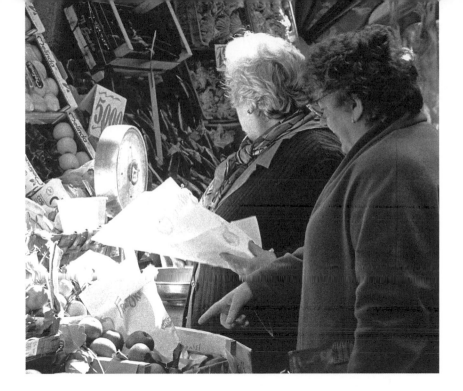

ALICI RIPIENE
Boned & stuffed anchovies

Fresh anchovies deteriorate quickly, so, if you do not live beside the sea where these prized little fish are caught, you may be out of luck. If you cannot find fresh anchovies, you can buy unsalted anchovies already filleted and preserved in oil – try your local fishmonger. In this typical family recipe from the Sorrento coast, the fresh tang of the stuffing contrasts wonderfully with the crisp battered fish.

✢ SERVES 4

1 kg (2¹/₄ lb) fresh anchovy fillets
4 garlic cloves, finely chopped
handful of fresh flat-leaf parsley,
  roughly chopped
50 g (1³/₄ oz) pecorino cheese, grated
plain flour for dredging
5 eggs, beaten
oil for frying
salt and freshly ground black pepper
3 lemons, cut into wedges, to serve

Rinse the anchovies and slit in half lengthways. Remove the bones and rinse the anchovy halves. Lay half of the anchovies skin-side down on a working surface. Make a stuffing by combining the garlic, parsley and cheese. Season with salt and black pepper. Spread a little of the stuffing over each anchovy, then cover each one with one of the remaining anchovy halves, skin-side up, to make little 'sandwiches'. Press down well.

Heat enough oil for shallow-frying in a heavy frying pan over a medium heat. When the oil is the correct temperature, dredge the anchovy sandwiches in a little flour, then dip in the beaten eggs. Carefully lower into the pan, and shallow-fry on both sides in the hot oil, cooking in batches if necessary. Cook for 15–20 minutes until the skin is crisp and the fish is just cooked through. Serve immediately, with the lemon wedges for squeezing over the top.

FROM THE SEA

A wealth of fantastic fish and seafood is found all along Campania's coastline, drawn from the Tyrrhenian Sea and the Bay of Naples. Long a source of food for the region's inhabitants, the bounty of the sea has become an intrinsic part of its distinctive cuisine. Red mullet, grey mullet, sea bream, tuna, anchovies, sardines, mackerel, clams, mussels, cuttlefish, squid, octopus – all these and more make their way from fishermen's nets and baskets to the fish markets and then onto the dining table. Yet even here, in the past, a clear division could be seen between the food of the rich and the poor. While the noble and wealthy families dined on the more prized white fish, such as red mullet and bream, and shellfish, such as oysters, poorer inhabitants made the most of what was considered to be inferior.

Clams, mussels, grey mullet, anchovies and sardines, among others, became characteristic and much-loved ingredients of *cucina povera*. Today, of course, what began as necessity is now very much a proud tradition; fish and seafood that were once chosen because of financial hardship are now eaten not only because of historical and cultural tradition, but also because of their quality and flavour. On any given day in the fish markets, you will find eager and discerning customers carefully making their selections, inspecting and questioning to make sure that they are buying the freshest squid or the firmest fish.

There was another historical division in the food, though, and that was between sea and land. Certainly, fish and seafood were staples of the diet for island and coastal dwellers. Away from the coast, however, it was a different story. In the mountains of Benevento and Avellino, for instance, seafood hardly appeared in the diet at all, except in the form of preserved fish such as anchovies or baccalà (salt cod) – perhaps this is one of the reasons why, even in times of modern refrigeration, salt cod is still widely eaten throughout Campania when it is now relatively easy to buy fresh fish. Salt cod at Christmas is a particular tradition that continues to this day.

A common thread running throughout the preparation of fish is simplicity. Fresh fish, such as bream, tend to be baked or grilled whole and are in the main simply dressed with olive oil, garlic and parsley. The same applies to seafood, such as mussels and clams. Even when ingredients like tomatoes appear, they never overwhelm the dish, allowing the flavour of the seafood to shine through.

FRITTURA DI CALAMARI E SCAMPI
Fried squid & scampi

Although sometimes synonymous with prawns, scampi are actually a type of lobster; in cooking, scampi generally refers to the peeled tail section. If you cannot find scampi for this traditional Neapolitan dish, substitute whole prawns instead, deveined but with the unpeeled tail left intact.

✢ SERVES 4

500 g (1 lb 2 oz) squid
500 g (1 lb 2 oz) scampi such
  as Norway lobster or Dublin
  Bay prawns
plain flour for dredging
vegetable oil for frying
salt and freshly ground black pepper
lemon wedges, to serve

Clean the squid and cut into rings (see page 16). Wash and clean the scampi. Dredge the squid and scampi in the flour, shaking off any excess. Heat plenty of oil for deep-frying in a large frying pan over a medium heat. Carefully drop in the squid and scampi, cooking in batches so that you do not crowd the pan. Fry for 5 minutes until golden. Drain on kitchen paper, and sprinkle with salt and black pepper. Serve piping hot, with lemon wedges for squeezing over the top.

SOUTÈ DI VONGOLE
Clams sautéed in garlic & oil

Another classic Neapolitan recipe, this one uses the abundant clams found along Campania's coastline.

✢ SERVES 4

2 kg (4¹/₂ lb) carpet shell clams
2 tablespoons olive oil
5 garlic cloves, finely chopped
generous handful of fresh flat-leaf
  parsley, chopped
salt and freshly ground black pepper

Rinse the clams and leave to soak in salted water for a few hours to release any grit (see note on page 42). Rinse well under cold running water. Tap on a work surface and discard any that do not close or have broken shells.

    Heat the oil in a heavy saucepan over a medium heat, and sweat the garlic for a few minutes until soft and starting to caramelize. Add the clams and a good sprinkling of black pepper. Cover the pan and sauté the clams, shaking the pan occasionally, until they open (discard any that do not open). Transfer to a serving bowl, sprinkle the clams generously with chopped parsley and serve immediately.

CEFALO ARROSTO
Grilled marinated grey mullet

Grey mullet is a popular catch in the Bay of Naples, and this traditional fisherman's recipe is typical of those from the Borgo Santa Lucia area of Naples, the city's old fishing quarter.

✛ SERVES 4

2 kg (4½ lb) grey mullet
2 tablespoons olive oil
1–2 tablespoons balsamic vinegar
4 garlic cloves, finely chopped
handful of fresh flat-leaf parsley,
  leaves picked and chopped
2 fresh sage leaves, chopped
2 sprigs of fresh rosemary, leaves
  picked and chopped
5 slices crustless stale Italian bread
  such as ciabatta or pane casereccio,
  broken up into large crumbs
salt
3 lemons, cut into slices, to serve

Clean the fish and cut a slit through the belly. Remove the innards and the bones (you can ask your fishmonger to do this). Combine the oil, vinegar, garlic, parsley, sage and rosemary in a small bowl. Drench the bread in the herb mixture. Stuff the cavity in each fish with the bread mixture, and secure with a toothpick or cocktail stick.

Heat a barbecue or charcoal grill, or a ridged grill pan, until medium hot. Arrange the fish on the grill and cook, brushing continually with the excess marinade and turning frequently, for 25–30 minutes. Be careful not to overcook. Serve the fish with slices of lemon.

CEFALO ALLA MARINARA
Grey mullet with spring onion & parsley

Given its long history, it is only natural that most dishes originating in Borgo Santa Lucia should centre on the bounty of the sea. Once again, grey mullet is the fish of choice, but this time it is cooked whole in a simple fresh herb sauce.

✛ SERVES 4

2 kg (4½ lb) grey mullet
about 1 tablespoon olive oil
500 g (1 lb 2 oz) spring onions,
  green part only, finely sliced on
  the diagonal
generous handful fresh flat-leaf
  parsley, leaves picked and roughly
  chopped
salt and freshly ground black pepper

Clean the fish (you can ask your fishmonger to do this), and arrange in a heavy frying pan. Drizzle with the oil, then sprinkle the spring onions and parsley over the fish. Season with salt and black pepper. Add about 250 ml (8 fl oz) water, and simmer over a gentle heat for 30 minutes until the fish is cooked through; add a little extra water if necessary as the fish is cooking, to keep it from drying out. Serve hot, with the fish juices served separately.

TRIGLIE DEL PESCATORE
Grilled marinated red mullet

Red mullet are a delicate, flaky fish that work very well when grilled or barbecued. Marinating the fish before grilling, and then basting again with the marinade during the cooking process, improves their flavour even more. This time the recipe comes from Borgo Marinari, a traditional fishing village in the old Santa Lucia quarter sitting right on the water's edge.

✥ SERVES 4

4 tablespoons olive oil
3 garlic cloves, finely chopped
generous handful of fresh flat-leaf
  parsley, roughly chopped
juice of 2 lemons plus 1 tablespoon
  extra for grilling
6 whole red mullet, cleaned (you can
  ask your fishmonger to do this)
2 or 3 fresh mint leaves, chopped
salt and freshly ground black pepper

Prepare a marinade with half of the oil, the garlic, parsley and juice of 2 lemons. Season well with salt and black pepper. Lay the fish in a single layer in a shallow glass or ceramic dish, and leave to marinate in the refrigerator for at least an hour.

Heat a ridged grill pan or heavy frying pan over a medium heat. Make a separate marinade for brushing the fish with the remaining oil, the extra lemon juice and the mint. Season with salt and black pepper. Once the pan is hot, grill the fish for 3–4 minutes on each side until just cooked through, brushing frequently with the marinade. (Be careful not to overcook; otherwise the flesh will be dry.) Serve immediately.

Note If you choose to barbecue the fish or cook them over a charcoal grill, you may find it easier to use a wire fish rack to cook them in, as these fish are so delicate. This helps to prevent them breaking up or losing their tails.

SPIGOLA AL FORNO
Baked sea bass with oil & lemon

Sea bass is another typical fish found in Naples' markets and fishmongers. In this recipe, it is treated with the simple reverence that is fundamental in so much of Neapolitan cuisine.

✥ SERVES 4

3 garlic cloves, finely chopped
handful of fresh flat-leaf parsley,
  leaves picked and chopped
2 tablespoons olive oil
1 large sea bass (about 1.25 kg/2¾ lb)
  or 2 small ones, cleaned and scaled
juice of 2 lemons
salt

Preheat the oven to 150°C (300°F/Gas 2). In a small bowl, mix the garlic and parsley with half of the oil. Season with salt, and use the mixture to stuff the fish. Place in a fish pan, and drizzle with the remaining oil. Bake in the oven for 15 minutes, then add the lemon juice. Bake for a further 15 minutes, transfer to a serving platter and serve hot.

SEPPIE IMBOTTITE
Squid stuffed with shellfish & bread

You would expect a dish from Naples' Borgo Marinari district to make the very best of a fisherman's daily catch. On almost any given day, if you walk down to the shoreline in Naples, you will find fishermen sorting and selling fish and seafood almost straight from the sea – and often still wriggling, which is a guarantee of freshness. The squid used in this recipe is kept moist and succulent as it cooks by the seafood-studded bread stuffing, then smothered in a smooth chilli-spiked tomato sauce.

✚ SERVES 4

6 large squid
4 tablespoons olive oil
500 g (1 lb 2 oz) raw prawns, peeled and deveined
2 eggs
1 tablespoon freshly grated pecorino cheese
500 g (1 lb 2 oz) stale good-quality bread such as ciabatta or pane casereccio, crusts removed
1 fresh red chilli, deseeded and finely chopped
2 garlic cloves, finely chopped
800 g (1³/₄ lb) ripe tomatoes, peeled and chopped
salt and freshly ground black pepper
generous handful of fresh flat-leaf parsley, leaves picked and chopped, to serve

Clean the squid well, removing the eyes, ink sacs and beaks (see page 16) so that you are left with a long tube. Heat 2 tablespoons of the oil in a heavy frying pan over a medium heat, and sauté the prawns for 5–8 minutes, depending on size, until they turn pink and opaque. Remove from the pan, chop into small pieces and set aside in a bowl.

Soak the bread in a little water, then gently squeeze out any excess liquid. Whisk the eggs with the pecorino and bread. Season with salt and black pepper, and add to the prawns. Mix the filling well, and use it to stuff the squid. Tie up the open ends with butcher's string or cotton thread.

Heat the remaining oil in a large heavy pan over a medium heat, and sweat the garlic with the chilli for a few minutes until soft and starting to caramelize. Add the squid and quickly sauté until golden brown, then add the tomatoes, cover the pan and leave for 20 minutes to cook through, stirring occasionally. Remove the squid from the pan, snip off the string and set the squid aside. Quickly push the tomato sauce through a sieve to ensure it is smooth. Serve the stuffed squid hot, cut into slices, accompanied by the tomato sauce and a good sprinkling of chopped parsley.

BACCALÀ ALLA NAPOLETANA
Salt cod fillets with tomato, olives & capers

The classic Neapolitan triumvirate of tomatoes, olives and capers adds its characteristic piquancy to this simple dish, as well as providing layers of texture and depth.

✤ SERVES 4

1 kg (2¼ lb) salt cod

4 tablespoons olive oil

3 garlic cloves, finely chopped

500 g (1 lb 2 oz) ripe tomatoes, peeled, deseeded and chopped (see note on page 116)

150 g (5 oz) black olives, pitted and left whole or halved

50 g (1¾ oz) salted capers, rinsed and gently squeezed dry

plain flour for dredging

generous handful of fresh flat-leaf parsley, leaves picked and chopped

salt and freshly ground black pepper

Soak the salt cod in several changes of cold fresh water overnight.

The next day, preheat the oven to 150°C (300°F/Gas 2). Heat half of the oil in a large heavy pan over a medium heat. Sweat the garlic for a few minutes until soft and starting to colour. Using a slotted spoon, remove the garlic from the pan, leaving the oil behind. Add the tomatoes, olives and capers. Season with a little salt and a generous grinding of black pepper. Cook over a gentle heat for 10–15 minutes until the tomatoes start to break down.

In the meantime, drain the salt cod and rinse well under cold running water. Remove and discard any bones or skin, then pat the salt cod dry with kitchen paper. Cut into pieces and coat in a little flour. Heat the remaining oil in a separate large heavy pan over a medium heat, and quickly fry the cod until golden on all sides. Remove from the pan with a slotted spoon, and drain on kitchen paper.

Return the cod to the same pan as the tomato mixture, and sprinkle in the parsley. Cook for a few more minutes, then transfer to an ovenproof dish and bake in the preheated oven for 10 minutes. Serve hot.

BACCALÀ ALLA FRANCESE
Salt cod with onion & wine

Mussillo is a whole piece of salt cod taken from the centre of the fish. It is left whole and gently simmered in the onion and wine sauce until tender.

✤ SERVES 4

1 kg (2¼ lb) mussillo of salt cod (the centre cut of the cod)

1 onion, sliced

2 tablespoons olive oil

pinch of salt

2 glasses of dry white wine

2 litres (3½ pints) boiling water

generous handful of fresh flat-leaf parsley, leaves picked and chopped

freshly ground black pepper

Soak the salt cod in several changes of cold fresh water overnight.

The next day, rinse the salt cod well under running water, pat dry with kitchen paper and put in a large heavy pan with the onion, oil and a pinch of salt. Season with black pepper. Sweat over a medium heat for about 10 minutes, turning the cod over halfway during cooking. Pour over the wine and cook for a further 5 minutes until the wine has reduced completely.

Add the boiling water and simmer gently, uncovered, for 30 minutes. When the fish looks tender, add a good sprinkling of chopped parsley, cook for a further 5 minutes and serve hot.

BOCCONCINI DEL PRETE
Baked mini omelettes with provolone, ham & tomato

Bocconcini means 'delicacies' – in this case, priests' delicacies. This is another convent recipe that makes the most of a few premium ingredients. Here, the sweet, acidic intensity of the tomato topping cuts through the richness of the provolone cheese and ham to provide a perfect balance.

✤ SERVES 4

700 g (1 lb 9 oz) tinned whole peeled
  plum tomatoes
about 2 tablespoons olive oil
50 g (1³/4 oz) dried oregano
12 eggs
100 g (3¹/2 oz) Parmesan cheese,
  grated
200 g (7 oz) Italian cooked
  ham, sliced
200 g (7 oz) provola affumicata
  (smoked provolone cheese), sliced
salt and freshly ground black pepper

Preheat the oven to 150°C (300°F/Gas 2). Roughly chop the tomatoes and put in a pan with their juices. Add a little oil and the oregano, and season with salt and black pepper. Cook gently over a medium heat, stirring occasionally, until the tomatoes break up and reduce into a thick sauce.

Beat the eggs with a little salt and the Parmesan. Place a small omelette pan or similar over a medium heat, and make 8 small equal-sized omelettes using the egg mixture. (If you do not have a pan that is small enough, you could use an extra-large round biscuit cutter about 10 cm/4 in or so in diameter to contain your omelettes initially, while they start to set.) Do not fold over and do not allow the egg to set completely. Carefully slide them out of the pan with a spatula, and arrange half of the omelettes side by side in a baking dish. Put some ham and some provolone on top of each one. Cover with another little omelette, and pour over the tomato sauce. Bake in the oven for a few minutes until the cheese starts to melt. Serve hot.

FRITTO DI MOZZARELLA E PROVOLA
Mozarella & provolone fritters

Provolone is very much a Southern Italian cheese, even if today much of it is produced in the north of the country. It makes the perfect companion for that quintessentially Campanian cheese, mozzarella, in these traditional fritters that are often sold as street food in Naples.

✤ SERVES 4

250 g (9 oz) buffalo mozzarella
  cheese, cut into slices
250 g (9 oz) provola affumicata
  (smoked provolone cheese), sliced
plain flour for dredging
250 g (9 oz) good-quality dried
  breadcrumbs (see note on page 19)
vegetable oil for shallow-frying

Dredge the mozzarella and provolone slices in the flour, then dip in the beaten egg and finally in the breadcrumbs.

Heat enough oil for shallow-frying in a heavy pan over a medium heat. When the oil is hot, shallow-fry the cheese fritters for about 5 minutes until the coating is crisp and golden, and the cheese is melting inside. Carefully turn halfway during the cooking time using an egg slice or spatula, then lift out of the pan to drain briefly on kitchen paper once cooked. It is important to serve these virtually straight from the frying pan to the table – *frienn' magnann'*. Serve hot, with a warning to guests about the hot cheese inside.

FRITTATA DI PATATE
Potato frittata

Frittate make a perfect family meal or easy lunch or supper dish, and they really could not be easier to make. Three recipes for frittata are actually given here, and all make use of simple but high-quality produce for the best results.

1 tablespoon olive oil
1 kg (2¼ lb) waxy potatoes, peeled and cut into cubes
8 large eggs
500 ml (16 fl oz) milk
1–2 tablespoons freshly grated Parmesan cheese plus extra for sprinkling (optional)
generous handful of fresh flat-leaf parsley, leaves picked and chopped
100 g (3½ oz) butter
salt and freshly ground black pepper

Heat the oil in a large frying pan over a medium heat, and sauté the potatoes for 15 minutes until golden. Don't cook completely – just until they are starting to colour and soften slightly inside. Otherwise they will break up when you add them to the frittata mixture. Drain on kitchen paper and leave to cool.

In the meantime, put the eggs, milk, the 1–2 tablespoons Parmesan cheese and the parsley in a large bowl. Season with salt and black pepper, and whisk until the mixture is well combined and the eggs are light and fluffy. Add the potato and gently stir through to mix well.

To cook the frittata, melt the butter in a frying pan over a medium heat. Carefully pour in the egg mixture. Continue cooking until the bottom is set and golden brown. Using a metal spatula or egg slice, slip the frittata out onto a plate, right-side up. Return to the pan right-side down, and cook for a few more minutes until set. If you like, cook the bottom of the frittata in the frying pan on the stove, then finish off under a hot grill, sprinkling the top with a little extra Parmesan before you do so. Be careful not to overcook – the egg continues cooking after you remove it from the heat. Leave in the pan until set firmly enough to slide out using a spatula or egg slice. Serve warm or cold, cut into slices, accompanied by a fresh green salad or vegetable side dish.

Frittata di spinaci Blanch 300 g (10 oz) spinach in boiling water for a couple of minutes until just wilted. (The length of time you need to do this depends on the age of the leaves; very young spinach leaves will wilt in hardly any time at all.) Drain well using a colander, then gently squeeze out any excess water from the spinach and chop finely. Heat 2 tablespoons of olive oil in a heavy frying pan over a medium heat. Sauté the spinach for a minute or so until coated in the oil. Beat 5 large eggs with 2 tablespoons freshly grated Parmesan cheese. Season with salt and black pepper, then pour over the spinach. Mix gently, then continue cooking as for the potato frittata. SERVES 4

Frittata di cipolle Peel and finely slice 1 kg (2¼ lb) sweet onions. Soak in a bowl of cold water for 1 hour. Drain. Heat 2 tablespoons of olive oil in a heavy frying pan over a medium heat. Sweat the onions for 20–30 minutes, stirring often, until soft and caramelized. Beat 10 large eggs with 100 g (3½ oz) freshly grated Parmesan cheese. Season with salt and black pepper. When the onion is soft, pour the egg mixture over the top. Mix through gently, then continue cooking as for the potato frittata. SERVES 4

CONTORNI
Side dishes

FAGIOLINI INDORATI E FRITTI
Fried green beans

Choose the freshest beans you can find for this classic dish, typically sold in *friggitoria*, where the food goes literally straight from frying pan to table – or *frienn' magnann'*, as they say in the local dialect. The sweetness of the crisp beans contrasts perfectly with the Parmesan-flavoured batter.

SERVES 4

500 g (1 lb 2 oz) fresh green beans, ends trimmed if necessary
light olive oil for shallow-frying
3 eggs
50 g (1³/4 oz) Parmesan cheese, freshly grated
plain flour for dredging
salt

Blanch the beans in boiling salted water for a few minutes until just tender, but still with a bite. Drain, then put in a colander and rinse under cold running water to refresh (you want them to keep their bright-green colour). Leave to cool while you prepare the coating.

Heat enough oil for shallow-frying in a heavy pan over a medium heat. Beat the eggs with a little salt and the Parmesan cheese. When the oil is hot, quickly coat the beans in the flour and dip a few at a time into the egg mixture. Carefully drop them into the oil one by one, cooking in batches of three or four so that the temperature of the oil does not drop during cooking. Fry for a couple of minutes until golden, remove with a slotted spoon and drain on kitchen paper. Repeat the process until all the beans have been used. Keep a production line going so that the beans are still crisp, piping hot and at their best when they reach the table. Serve immediately.

FAGIOLI IN UMIDO
Stewed beans in cherry tomato sauce

Fresh beans are best for this classic recipe, but you could use dried beans if fresh ones are not available. You will need to soak dried beans overnight in plenty of cold water with a pinch of bicarbonate of soda, then rinse well before cooking. Variations of this dish are found throughout Italy – some are made with cannellini beans and sage; others use lentils.

SERVES 4

3 tablespoons olive oil
1 kg (2¹/4 lb) fresh cannellini or borlotti beans, shelled
2 garlic cloves, finely chopped
1 celery stick, roughly chopped
1 fresh red chilli, deseeded and finely chopped
50 g (1³/4 oz) fresh cherry tomatoes, cut into quarters
2 teaspoons dried oregano
salt and freshly ground black pepper

Heat 2 tablespoons of the oil in a heavy pan over a medium heat. Add the beans, half the garlic and the celery, and sweat for a few minutes. Pour in just enough water to come about halfway up the beans, bring to a simmer, then cover the pan. Reduce the heat and simmer gently, stirring occasionally, for about 1 hour until the beans are tender but not mushy (adding extra water if necessary). Once they start to soften, season with salt and pepper. Just before the end of the cooking time, heat the remaining 1 tablespoon oil in a separate large pan over a medium heat. Sweat the remaining garlic and the chilli for a few minutes until soft and starting to colour. Add the tomatoes and cook down for 5 minutes. Drain the beans, and pick out and discard the celery. Add the beans to the tomato sauce. Check the seasoning, adding more salt if necessary, and sprinkle in the oregano. Stir through well and cook for a further 5 minutes so that the flavours develop and meld. Serve immediately.

COFFEE CULTURE

Coffee is much more than a drink in Naples. In fact, drinking coffee is in many ways more of a pastime, and it is certainly steeped in ritual. If it is going to be proper coffee, most Neapolitans will tell you, it should be made from Arabica beans. Purists also say that to make a real cup of coffee at home you need a *caffettiera napoletana*, or Neapolitan drip-coffee pot. Traditionally made of metal, this is a nineteenth-century predecessor of the octagonal *moka* coffee pot. Like the *moka*, it comes in two parts, and is separated by a coffee filter. The bottom half is filled with water, then coffee grounds are lightly packed into the filter and the top replaced. The pot is put onto the heat to boil; as soon as the water starts to boil, the pot is removed from the heat and the coffee pot flipped upside down, allowing the water to filter slowly through the coffee. True aficionados will place a metal cover, a piece of foil or a twist of newspaper – known as a *coppetiello* in the Neapolitan dialect – in the spout to keep the coffee hot and prevent the aromatic steam escaping. Alfonso Bialetti's *moka caffettiera* is still commonly used, and those unwilling to wait for their coffee to drip through a *napoletana* always have at least one of these on hand.

Cafés and bars serving fine espresso coffee abound in Naples, and Neapolitans take the act of drinking a coffee at one of these establishments very seriously – in many cases they do so several times a day. It is this devotion to good coffee that has made Naples Italy's coffee-drinking capital. First, there is the question of what style of coffee to choose: a shot of *espresso*, a *caffè macchiato* (with a dash of milk), a *latte macchiato* (steamed milk with a dash of coffee, considered a breakfast drink or for those not up to drinking 'real' coffee), or a *cappuccino* (espresso with whipped steamed milk). Even here there are variations, as a *cappuccino* can come with froth or without, and be either cold, warm or piping hot. Expert preparation of coffee is considered a fine art, and watching a white-jacketed Neapolitan barman preparing a cup leaves you in no doubt that this is absolutely true.

Neapolitans throng to the city's many coffee bars day and night, and everyone has their own favourite. Still, it is hard to go past the Caffè Gambrinus, which has been serving coffee for 150 years and whose customers have included Guy de Maupassant and Oscar Wilde, without entering its ornate interior for a traditional cup.

INSALATA CAPRESE
Tomato, basil & mozzarella salad

On a summer's day, what could be more perfect than this classic salad from the island of Capri, with its fabulous marriage of choice ingredients, fresh flavours and aromas.

✢ SERVES 4

500 g (1 lb 2 oz) flavourful ripe
  plum or round salad tomatoes, cut
  into slices
good-quality extra virgin olive oil
  for drizzling
500 g (1 lb 2 oz) mozzarella cheese,
  cut into round slices
small handful of fresh oregano leaves
large bunch of fresh basil,
  leaves picked
salt and freshly ground black pepper

Layer the tomatoes on a platter or in a shallow serving dish. Season with salt and drizzle with a little oil. Arrange the slices of mozzarella over the slices of tomato. Sprinkle with the oregano and scatter over the basil leaves. Season well with black pepper and serve.

INSALATA DI FAGIOLI
White bean salad with tuna, spring onion & olives

Another classic summertime dish, this simple Neapolitan salad once again makes the most of a few choice ingredients. This time it combines elements of sea and land, with the saltiness of the tuna and olives providing a counterpoint to the sweet cannellini beans and tart dressing.

✢ SERVES 4

500 g (1 lb 2 oz) fresh cannellini or
  borlotti beans, shelled
200-g (7-oz) jar tuna in oil, drained
  and flaked
3 spring onions, green parts only,
  finely sliced on the diagonal
50 g (1³/4 oz) black olives, pitted
fresh flat-leaf parsley, leaves picked
  and chopped
1 tablespoon good-quality balsamic
  vinegar
2 tablespoons extra virgin olive oil
salt and freshly ground black pepper

Put the beans in a saucepan and cover with cold water. Bring to the boil and simmer gently for 15–20 minutes until tender but still whole. Drain and transfer to a serving bowl. Add the tuna, spring onions and olives. Drizzle over the vinegar and oil, sprinkle in the parsley and season with salt and black pepper. Toss gently but well. Cover and leave in the refrigerator for a couple of hours, to allow the flavours to develop before serving.

CARCIOFI E PATATE
Braised artichokes & potatoes

Artichokes are a very popular vegetable in Campania and grow abundantly. Fresh or preserved, they are used throughout the year in dishes ranging from simple antipasti and soups, to pasta and side dishes. In this classic Neapolitan recipe, fresh artichokes are gently braised with potatoes, in the same delicious combination as in the potato and artichoke soup on page 28.

✤ SERVES 4

5 fresh artichokes
4 floury potatoes
4 tablespoons olive oil
generous handful of fresh flat-leaf
  parsley, or to taste, leaves picked
  and chopped
2 garlic cloves, peeled and
  lightly crushed
salt and freshly ground black pepper

Clean the artichokes well, removing the tough outer leaves. Using a teaspoon, remove and discard the central choke and any prickly inner leaves. Cut the artichokes into quarters. Peel the potatoes and cut into wedges. Heat the oil in a non-stick frying pan over a medium heat, and sweat the garlic for a few minutes until soft and golden. Remove the garlic from the pan using a slotted spoon, and add the artichokes and potatoes. Quickly sweat in the pan for a few minutes until they are coated with the garlic-infused oil. Pour in enough water so that the vegetables are just covered. Leave to cook, with the pan half covered, for about 25 minutes. Make sure that the liquid has reduced completely before removing from the heat. Serve hot, sprinkled with parsley.

ZUCCHETTE E PATATE
Baby zucchini & potato stew

Courgettes thrive in Campania's fertile soil and mild climate, and are a staple of *cucina povera*, the cuisine which led to Neapolitans being known as *mangiafoglie* (leaf eaters). This particular recipe is traditionally served at Easter, along with several other signature dishes such as the more elaborate *minestra di Pasqua*, but works well at any time when baby courgettes are in season.

✤ SERVES 4

500 g (1 lb 2 oz) potatoes
a little olive oil
1 onion, finely chopped
1 celery stick, chopped
1.5 kg (3 lb 3 oz) baby courgettes, cut
  into largish pieces
salt and freshly ground black pepper
small handful of fresh flat-leaf
  parsley, leaves picked and chopped,
  to garnish

Peel the potatoes and cut into wedges. Heat a little olive oil in a pan over a medium heat. Add the potatoes, onion and celery, and sweat until coated in the oil. Pour in just enough water to come about halfway up the potatoes, bring to a simmer and cover the pan. Reduce the heat, and continue cooking gently for 20 minutes, stirring occasionally, until the potatoes are nearly cooked. Add the courgettes and continue cooking, covered, for a further 5 minutes until the liquid has reduced and the vegetables are done – be careful not to let the courgettes become too mushy. Season with salt and black pepper, and scatter the parsley over the top. Serve hot.

ZUCCHINE UOVA E FORMAGGIO
Courgettes with eggs, pancetta & Parmesan

Many people think of courgettes as being bland and watery, but the key is to choose courgettes that are not too large and to combine them with other ingredients that enhance their flavour, as is the case in this simple yet delicious Easter recipe.

✤ SERVES 4

2 tablespoons olive oil
1 onion, finely chopped
50 g (1³/₄ oz) pancetta, cut into
   1-cm (¹/₂-in) dice
1 kg (2¹/₄ lb) courgettes, cut into
   1-cm (¹/₂-in) dice
3 eggs
1–2 tablespoons freshly grated
   Parmesan cheese
handful of fresh flat-leaf parsley,
   leaves picked and chopped
salt and freshly ground black pepper

Heat the oil in a pan over a medium heat. Sweat the onion and pancetta until the onion is soft and starting to caramelize. Add the courgettes and season with salt and black pepper. Pour over 250 ml (8 fl oz) water, cover and leave to cook gently for 15 minutes.

In the meantime, beat the eggs with a pinch of salt, the Parmesan and the parsley. As soon as the courgettes are cooked, add the beaten eggs and stir rapidly. Remove from the heat before the eggs are completely set, and serve straight away.

MELANZANE IN CARROZZA
Fried aubergine & provolone sandwiches

Hailing from the region around Mount Vesuvius, this recipe is another example of how to prepare food *in carrozza*, or 'in a carriage' (see page 17). This time, aubergines sandwich slices of *provola*, or provolone, a semi-hard cheese which is a speciality of Campania.

✤ SERVES 4

1.5 kg (3 lb 3 oz) aubergines
olive oil for shallow-frying
500 g (1 lb 2 oz) unsmoked provolone
   cheese, cut into slices about 1 cm
   (¹/₂ in) thick
plain flour for dredging
5 eggs, beaten
salt and freshly ground black pepper

Cut the aubergines into round slices about 1 cm (½ in) thick. Sprinkle with salt, place in a colander, put a weight on the top and leave for about an hour to drain off any bitterness and excess liquid.

Rinse the aubergines well, pat dry with a clean tea towel or kitchen paper, and shallow-fry in very hot oil for about 5 minutes until starting to turn a golden colour. Turn over and cook on the other side for a few more minutes. Drain on kitchen paper to remove any excess oil.

Place a slice of provola between 2 slices of the aubergine. Quickly dredge in the flour, dip in the beaten eggs and shallow-fry in very hot oil until golden brown. Season with salt and black pepper, and serve piping hot.

PARMIGIANA DI MELANZANE
Baked aubergines with tomatoes & mozzarella

Possibly one of Naples' best known traditional dishes, and taken all over the world by the waves of migrants seeking a new life after World War II, *parmigiana di melanzane* is as tasty as it is familiar. Salting the aubergines before cooking them is the key to success – otherwise you will end up with a watery dish that falls apart when sliced. It is also important to press each layer down well when you are assembling the ingredients for baking.

✣ SERVES 4

1 kg (2¼ lb) large aubergines
olive oil for cooking
1 garlic clove, finely chopped
1 kg (2¼ lb) ripe tomatoes,
    preferably plum, peeled and chopped
    (see note)
300 g (10 oz) mozzarella cheese
60–75 g (2–3 oz) Parmesan
    cheese, grated
3 or 4 large fresh basil leaves,
    finely sliced
salt and freshly ground black pepper

Cut the aubergines into thickish slices. Sprinkle with salt and leave in a colander, preferably overnight, to draw out the excess water. Rinse and pat dry with kitchen paper. Heat enough light olive oil for shallow-frying in a pan over a medium-high heat, and add the aubergine slices in a single layer. Shallow-fry on both sides for a few minutes until the slices are starting to brown slightly. Make sure that the oil is hot before adding the aubergines to the pan, so that they do not absorb too much oil. Remove from the pan with a slotted spoon and drain on kitchen paper.

Meanwhile, preheat the oven to 180°C (350°F/Gas 4). Make a tomato sauce by heating a little oil in a saucepan over a medium heat. Add the garlic and cook until soft and transparent, before adding the tomatoes and basil. Season with salt and black pepper. Cook down for 10 minutes until the tomatoes have broken up and reduced into a pulpy sauce.

As soon as the sauce is ready, arrange alternate layers of aubergines, tomato sauce, slices of mozzarella and Parmesan in a greased baking dish. Make sure that you press down the ingredients well, so that you end up with compacted layers in the finished dish. Finish off with a layer of sauce and a sprinkling of Parmesan. Bake in the preheated oven for about 40 minutes. Let stand for a few minutes to allow the ingredients to set slightly, then cut into individual portions while still in the dish. Carefully slide out onto serving plates using a spatula or egg slice, and serve hot.

Peeling tomatoes It is not such an onerous task, peeling fresh tomatoes. Simply score the skin slightly with a sharp knife, blanch in boiling water for 10 seconds or so until the skin starts to soften and split, then refresh in cold water. This makes it far easier to use a sharp knife to peel away the skin.

STUFATO DI VERDURE
Spicy ratatouille of peppers, aubergines & potatoes

Not surprisingly for a traditional convent recipe, given these institutions' history of growing market produce, this dish draws heavily on the basic premise of using fresh produce to its best advantage – in this case, a heady and colourful mélange of vegetables.

✣ SERVES 4

1 kg (2¼ lb) red and yellow peppers
700 g (1 lb 10 oz) floury potatoes
800 g (1¾ lb) aubergines
2 tablespoons olive oil
2 garlic cloves
3 onions, chopped
200 g (7 oz) ripe tomatoes, halved, deseeded and finely chopped
1 tablespoon finely chopped fresh oregano leaves or 2 teaspoons dried
2 or 3 large fresh basil leaves, or to taste, finely sliced
salt and freshly ground black pepper

Remove the stalk, seeds and membrane from the peppers, and cut into thin strips. Peel the potatoes and cut into 1-cm (½-in) dice. Dice the aubergines into a similar size.

Heat the oil in a pan over a medium heat, and sweat the onions and garlic for a few minutes until soft. Add the tomatoes and allow to cook down slightly, then add the peppers, aubergines and potatoes. Stir through to coat the vegetables in the oil, then season with salt, cover the pan and cook over a medium heat for about 30 minutes.

Remove the lid from the pan and cook the vegetable mixture for a few more minutes to allow the liquid to reduce. Sprinkle over the oregano and basil (if using dried oregano, you may wish to add it a little earlier while you are reducing the liquid, so that the flavour develops). Serve hot or cold.

CARCIOFI INDORATI E FRITTI
Deep-fried artichokes

Deep-fried artichokes are often served in Naples' *trattorie* and are just one of the array of *frienn' magnann'* (fry and eat) delicacies that are so much a part of the city's street and food life.

✣ SERVES 4

8 artichokes
juice of 1 lemon, to acidulate artichokes
3 eggs
60 g (2 oz) Parmesan cheese, grated
pinch of salt
100 g (3½ oz) plain or tipo 00 flour
light olive oil for deep-frying
sea salt, to serve

Remove the tough outer leaves from the artichokes. Snip the tops off the larger leaves. Leave to soak for 30 minutes in a bowl of water with the lemon juice. Using a teaspoon, remove the choke and any prickly inner leaves. Cut each artichoke into 4 wedges.

To make the batter for coating the artichokes, beat the eggs with the Parmesan and salt. Dredge the artichoke pieces in the flour, gently shake off any excess, then dip in the beaten egg. Deep-fry in batches in very hot oil for 5–10 minutes until golden brown, depending on the size of the artichokes. Remove with a slotted spoon and drain on kitchen paper. Serve piping hot, with a bowl of sea salt at the table for seasoning.

ZUCCHINE CON LA MOZZARELLA
Baked courgettes & mozzarella

Traditionally served at Easter, this dish is a fine example of layering and baking vegetables to bring out their flavour. This technique is a feature of Campanian cuisine, and conforms to the tenets of slow cooking found throughout the region and particularly in the revered *ragù*. Usually this type of dish would be made in a special clay pot, but a good ceramic baking dish will suffice.

⸙ SERVES 4

2 tablespoons olive oil

1 kg (2¼ lb) courgettes, cut into rounds

300 g (10 oz) buffalo mozzarella, cut into slices

1 2 tablespoons freshly grated Parmesan cheese

2 or 3 large fresh basil leaves, torn into small pieces

50 g (1¾ oz) butter

salt and freshly ground black pepper

Preheat the oven to 150°C (300°F/Gas 2). Heat the olive oil in a heavy pan over a medium heat. Add the courgettes and sauté for 5–10 minutes until starting to brown. Remove from the pan with a slotted spoon and drain briefly on kitchen paper.

Arrange a layer of courgettes in the bottom of a baking dish. Cover with a layer of mozzarella, sprinkle with some Parmesan and basil, and season with salt and black pepper. Repeat the process, finishing off with a layer of courgettes. Cover with some more grated Parmesan and dot with the butter. Bake in the preheated oven for 15 minutes and serve immediately.

PEPERONI IMBOTTITE
Roasted peppers stuffed with aubergine, olives & capers

The volcanic island of Ischia lies at the northern end of the Gulf of Naples, and it is from here that these exquisite stuffed peppers come. The peppers are char-grilled first, then their skins peeled off and the insides removed – this enhances their sweetness, so that they almost melt in your mouth and contrast beautifully with the textures and flavours of the piquant stuffing. *Peperoni imbottite* certainly deserve their place in the line-up of dishes that typify the cuisine of Naples and its surroundings. You can easily increase the quantities to make a larger amount if you wish.

✣ SERVES 4–6

6 red peppers
500 g (1 lb 2 oz) aubergines, cut into
   1-cm (1/2-in) dice
olive oil for cooking
6 slices of good-quality stale bread
   such as ciabatta or pane casereccio,
   cut into 1-cm (1/2-in) dice
85 g (3 oz) olives, pitted and halved
75 g (2 1/2 oz) salted capers, rinsed
   and squeezed dry
2 garlic cloves, finely chopped
2 salted anchovy fillets, chopped
handful of fresh flat-leaf parsley,
   leaves picked and chopped
salt and freshly ground black pepper

Preheat the oven to 150°C (300°F/Gas 2). Char the peppers over an open flame or under a hot grill until their skins are blistered and blackened in places. Carefully peel off the skin and discard. (Use rubber gloves if the peppers are too hot to handle, and if you like you can put them in a plastic bag for a few minutes after charring, to help make the skins easier to remove.) Carefully remove and discard the stem, central membrane and seeds, taking care to keep the peppers whole.

Heat a little olive oil in a frying pan over a medium heat. Add the aubergines and sauté for a few minutes until starting to brown. Remove from the pan with a slotted spoon, and drain on kitchen paper while you cook the bread. Using the same pan, gently fry the bread cubes until golden, adding a little extra oil if necessary.

Remove the croûtons from the pan and carefully mix with the aubergines, olives, capers, garlic, anchovies and parsley to make a stuffing. Season with salt and black pepper. Using a spoon, fill the peppers with the stuffing until they are nice and plump, and the stuffing is slightly mounded at the top. Arrange in a baking tin or dish, drizzle with extra olive oil and roast in the preheated oven for 20–25 minutes. Serve hot or cold.

PIZZA E PANE
Pizza & bread

WOOD-FIRED PIZZA

There is no doubt that Naples is the true home of pizza – all you need to do is ask a Neapolitan. It may have travelled around the world and now be found served in all sorts of variations, but its roots lie in very humble beginnings – that of the poor people who flocked to Naples in the early eighteenth century, looking for work and a place to live. Necessity is the mother of invention, and the pizza was originally little more than a dough of flour, water and salt, with a simple tomato topping. Although tomatoes had been brought back to Europe by the Portuguese after their travels to South America, they were long regarded as poisonous and only used as ornamental plants. It was not until the eighteenth century, particularly around Naples and Salerno, that they were cultivated for food.

It was not long before pizza had become a staple among the poor of Naples, and *pizzaioli* (pizza-makers) were selling their wares on the street, drawing visitors from outside into the poor areas to sample the dish. Officially, Naples' first pizzeria (pizzas were initially sold by people walking up and down the street touting freshly made pizza from nearby *pizzaiolo* kitchens), the Port 'Alba, opened in 1830; it still runs today and revels in its claim to being the first. The first pizza topping was the marinara. Despite the name, it contains no seafood, but instead is named for its popularity with the hungry fishermen who would readily devour this

dish at the end of a long night hauling in fish. It is, in fact, made with a tomato, garlic and oregano topping. Before long, the nobility and even the royal household became enamoured and the pizza became firmly implanted in Neapolitan cuisine. In 1889, Raffaele Esposito of the pizzeria Brandi (also still open today) invented the pizza Margherita, named in honour of the wife of King of Italy Umberto I. It is from these two original authentic toppings that all subsequent pizzas have come; by the end of the nineteenth century pizza could be eaten at any time of the day, bought from one of the many stalls and pizzerias built to cater to the seemingly incessant demand.

Neapolitans are so proud of the pizza – and certain devotees so determined to maintain its integrity – that there is even an organization dedicated to ensuring that it is made to the correct standards using traditional methods: the Associazione Vera Pizza Napoletana. Rules for an authentic pizza are: the dough must be made of flour, natural or brewer's yeast, salt and water only; the dough must be kneaded by hand (or by only those devices approved by the association); the pizza must be cooked directly on the oven floor; and it must be baked in a traditional bell-shaped wood-fired oven. There are more than 500 pizzerias in Naples: Port 'Alba, Brandi, Cafasso, da Michele, di Matteo, da Pasqualino, Trianon … the list goes on … and on.

PASTA PER PIZZE
Basic pizza dough

Making your own pizza dough is truly a simple task, and it provides you with a pizza base far superior to any shop-bought version. There is something so therapeutic about kneading dough that you will be in exactly the right frame of mind to devour your pizza when it is ready.

✣ MAKES ENOUGH FOR 4 LARGE PIZZAS

25 g (scant 1 oz) fresh yeast
500 ml (16 fl oz) warm water
1 kg (2 1/4 lb) strong plain white
  or tipo 0 flour
good pinch of salt

Dissolve the yeast in a little of the warm water. Sprinkle in a handful of the flour and mix well. Shape into a small ball and leave to rise in a dry place for 30 minutes. Make a well in the centre of the flour and add the yeast mixture, remaining warm water and a pinch of salt. Knead vigorously on a floured work surface for about 10 minutes, adding some warm water a little at a time until the dough is smooth but not sticky. Place on an oiled baking sheet and flatten out the dough with your hands, then cover with the topping of your choice. (You can freeze this dough to use later, but it is at its best when fresh.)

Pizza marinara This is the original and some would say the best, the roots from which all subsequent pizzas have sprung. To make 2 large pizzas, take ½ quantity of basic dough; shape into rounds. Using your knuckles, lightly press down around the edge of the dough about 3 cm (1 1/4 in) in from the edge, to make a slight rim. Drain 400 g (14 oz) tinned peeled plum tomatoes in a colander, pressing down gently to remove any excess juice. Roughly chop, then spread the tomato evenly over the dough, leaving a border of about 2 cm (1 in). Sprinkle over 2–3 thinly sliced garlic cloves and 2–3 teaspoons dried oregano. Drizzle generously with 3 tablespoons or so of olive oil. Season with salt and freshly ground black pepper. Slide onto an unglazed terracotta tile, pizza stone, pizza pan or baking sheet, and bake in the centre of a preheated oven at 230°–240°C (450°–475°F/Gas 8–9) for 8–10 minutes until crisp.

Pizza Margherita Pizza Margherita has its own special place in the hearts of Neapolitans. In 1889 Raffaele Esposito, a renowned *pizzaiolo* (pizza chef), named it after Queen Margherita, wife of Umberto I, King of Italy, during a visit the couple made to Naples. To make 2 large pizzas, take 1/2 quantity of basic dough and prepare as for pizza marinara. Drain 400 g (14 oz) tinned peeled plum tomatoes in a colander, pressing down gently to remove any excess juice. Roughly chop, then spread the tomato evenly over the dough, leaving a border of about 2 cm (1 in). Season with salt and drizzle generously with 2–3 tablespoons olive oil. Dot over 150g (5 oz) halved cherry tomatoes and 150–200 g (5–7 oz) drained sliced mozzarella cheese. Scatter over 10–12 finely sliced large fresh basil leaves. Sprinkle with a little grated Parmesan, if liked. Slide onto an unglazed terracotta tile, pizza stone, pizza pan or baking sheet, and bake in the centre of a preheated oven at 230°–240°C (450°–475°F/Gas 8–9) for 8–10 minutes until crisp.

CALZONE DI RICOTTA E SALAME
Ricotta & salami calzone

Calzone usually contains a filling based on a mixture of ricotta and mozzarella cheese. It makes for perfect street food, and in Naples kiosks and *trattorie* do a brisk business in this treat.

✣ SERVES 4–6

1/2 quantity of basic pizza dough
  (see page 129)
200 g (7 oz) fresh ricotta, drained
2 tablespoons freshly grated
  Parmesan cheese
100 g (3 1/2 oz) buffalo mozzarella
  cheese, diced
100 g (3 1/2 oz) spicy salami such as
  napoli or milano, diced
3 or 4 large fresh basil leaves, torn
a little extra virgin olive oil
freshly ground black pepper

Preheat the oven to 230°–240°C (450°–475°F/Gas 8–9). Prepare the basic pizza dough as on page 129. Put the ricotta, Parmesan, mozzarella and salami in a bowl. Sprinkle in the basil and season with black pepper. Mix until smooth and well combined. On a floured work surface, form the dough into a large round, and put the filling in a mound in the centre of the dough. Fold over in half to form a half-moon parcel. Press the edges together well so that the calzone is sealed tightly and the filling will not ooze out. Transfer to an oiled baking sheet, and drizzle a little oil over the calzone. Bake in the centre of the preheated oven for 8–12 minutes until crisp and golden.

Pizza fritta A Neapolitan speciality with a long tradition, *pizza fritta* is similar to calzone in that it is filled and the dough folded over on itself to form a parcel. The difference comes in the cooking. Instead of being baked, it is deep-fried in very hot oil or lard – definitely reserved for the very hungry.

PIZZA CON SALSICCIA PICCANTE E PATATE
Spicy sausage & potato pizza

This hearty and flavourful pizza is based on the principle of using few but quality ingredients.

✣ MAKES 2 LARGE PIZZAS OR
4 INDIVIDUAL ONES

1/2 quantity of basic pizza dough
  (see page 129)
about 150 g (5 oz) buffalo mozzarella
  cheese, sliced
300 g (10 oz) ripe cherry tomatoes,
  halved, or plum tomatoes, sliced
100 g (3 1/2 oz) new potatoes, sliced
100–150 g (3 1/2–5 oz) spicy Italian
  sausage such as salami napoli, sliced
3 or 4 sprigs of fresh rosemary, leaves
  picked and chopped
2 tablespoons extra virgin olive oil
sea salt

Prepare the pizza dough as on page 129. Flatten out with your hands into 2 large rounds, or divide the dough into 4 and make individual rounds. Using your knuckles, lightly press down around the edge of the dough about 2 cm (1 in) in from the edge, to make a slight rim. Top with the mozzarella slices. Dot around the cherry tomatoes, potato slices and spicy sausage. Sprinkle over the rosemary and season with sea salt. Drizzle the pizza with a little olive oil. Slide the pizza onto an unglazed tile, pizza stone, oiled pizza pan or oiled baking sheet. Bake in the centre of a preheated oven at 230°–240°C (450°–475°F/Gas 8–9) for 8–12 minutes until the base is crisp.

PIZZA CAPPERI, OLIVE E ACCIUGHE
Pizza with capers, olives & anchovies

Capers, olives and anchovies are three signature ingredients of Campanian cuisine, and of the cuisines of Southern Italy in general. They work well in combination, as seen in this classic pizza topping, with their strong, salty flavours cutting through the richness of the mozzarella and sweet tang of the cherry tomatoes.

✢ **MAKES 2 LARGE PIZZAS OR 4 INDIVIDUAL ONES**

½ quantity of basic pizza dough (see page 129)

300 g (10 oz) ripe cherry tomatoes, halved

about 150 g (5 oz) mozzarella cheese, sliced

25–30 anchovy fillets in olive oil, drained

about 4 tablespoons salted capers, rinsed and gently squeezed dry (you can be more generous with these if you like)

12–15 black olives such as Gaeta, pitted and chopped

2–3 teaspoons dried oregano

2–3 teaspoons extra virgin olive oil

Prepare the pizza dough as on page 129. Flatten out with your hands into 2 large rounds, or divide the dough into 4 and make individual rounds. Using your knuckles, lightly press down around the edge of the dough about 2 cm (1 in) in from the edge, to make a slight rim. Spread the tomatoes over the base of the pizza, leaving a border at the edge. Lay the anchovy fillets on top, spreading them around the base evenly. Sprinkle over the capers and olives, and scatter the oregano over the top. Drizzle the pizza with a little extra virgin olive oil (or you could use the drained oil from the anchovies if you like). Slide the pizza onto an unglazed tile, pizza stone, pizza pan or baking sheet, and bake in the centre of a preheated oven at 230°–240°C (450°–475°F/ Gas 8–9) for 8–12 minutes until the base is crisp.

IMPASTO PER PANE
Basic bread dough

The smell of baking bread is evocative of warmth and home. You can use this basic bread dough to make a rustic, country-style loaf or as the basis for breads such as the rosemary loaf below. Although similar to the classic sourdough *pane casereccio*, it is made without the *biga*, or starter, that is so much a part of the latter. Starters are an important part of Italian bread making; in some households the *biga* is kept going for years, ready to be used as the base of delicious homemade bread. With this recipe, though, you can make your own fresh crusty bread with relative ease.

⊹ MAKES 1 LARGE LOAF

25 g (1³/₄ oz) fresh yeast
300 ml (10 fl oz) warm water
500 g (1 lb 2 oz) plus 1¹/₂ tablespoons
 strong plain white or tipo 0 flour
2 teaspoons salt

Crumble the yeast into a bowl and dissolve in 200 ml (7 fl oz) of the warm water. Add the 1¹/₂ tablespoons of flour, mix together and shape into a soft round ball. Leave to rise in a warm place until it has doubled in size.

Make a well in the centre of the 500 g (1 lb 2 oz) flour and add the salt. Add enough of the remaining 100 ml (3 fl oz) warm water, a little at a time, to make a soft but not sticky dough. Add the yeast mixture; knead vigorously for about 20 minutes until the dough is soft and springy. Shape the dough into a ball, place in an oiled or buttered bowl, and make a cross-shaped cut in the top. Cover with a floured tea towel. Leave to rise at about 28°C (80°F) in a draught-free place, to prevent the top from drying out and forming a crust.

When the dough has doubled in size and leaves a dimple when you press lightly with your finger, knead again for a few minutes. Divide into portions, and shape as you wish. Bake on a lightly greased and floured baking sheet in a preheated oven at 240°C (475°F/Gas 9) for 40 minutes or until golden brown. The loaf should sound hollow when tapped on the bottom.

PANE AL ROSMARINO
Rosemary bread

Gently infusing the oil used in this bread with fresh rosemary means that the herb's distinctive flavour permeates the bread without being overpowering. You could experiment with fresh thyme instead, or other flavourings such as fennel seed, if you wish.

⊹ MAKES 4 SMALL LOAVES

1 quantity of basic bread dough
 (see above)
60 ml (2 fl oz) olive oil
2 or 3 sprigs of fresh rosemary,
 leaves picked
pinch of salt

Prepare the dough as above. Heat the oil in a small frying pan over a gentle heat. Add the rosemary, reserving 10 leaves. Soften over a gentle heat for 5 minutes, remove the sprigs and allow the oil to cool. Finely chop the reserved rosemary leaves. Add the rosemary-infused oil, chopped rosemary and a pinch of salt to the dough and knead well. Divide the dough into 4 small rounds, and leave to rise in a warm place for about 30 minutes. To bake, make a cross-shaped cut on the top of each loaf; brush with some of the leftover rosemary-infused oil. Bake in a preheated oven at 240°C (475°F/Gas 9) for 40 minutes or until golden brown. Remove from the oven and serve.

PANE DI OLIVE
Olive bread

Do not skimp on the olives you use in this delicious chewy bread, and avoid absolutely those that are sold already pitted – they are usually of an inferior quality. Just keep in mind the cornerstone of this regional cuisine: select the finest produce you can find for simple but stunning results.

✣ MAKES 1 LOAF

500 g (1 lb 2 oz) strong plain white
  or tipo 0 flour
pinch of salt
25 g (scant 1 oz) fresh yeast
250 ml (8 fl oz) warm water
100 g (3¹/₂ oz) butter, melted
about 150 g (5 oz) black olives such
  as Gaeta, pitted and halved

In a large bowl, mix the flour with a pinch of salt and make a well in the centre. Crumble the yeast into a small bowl, and dissolve in the warm water. Add the yeast liquid and combine well, adding a little more warm water if necessary. Transfer the dough to a floured work surface, and knead for about 10 minutes until the dough is firm and springy, working in the butter as you go. Shape into a ball, place in an oiled bowl and cover with a clean tea towel. Leave to rise for about 1 hour in a warm place.

When the dough has risen, knead again briefly and add the olives, mixing in well. Shape into a ball, replace in the oiled bowl and leave to rise once more, covered with a tea towel, for about 1¹/₂ hours or until cracks start to appear on the surface. Grease a baking sheet and flour lightly. Place the dough on the baking sheet and bake in a preheated oven at 240°C (475°F/Gas 9) for about 40 minutes or until the top is golden and the bread sounds hollow when knocked on the bottom. Remove from the oven and serve.

PANE DI NOCE
Walnut bread

Walnuts have grown in Campania for centuries, and from their original habitat on the Sorrento Peninsula they have spread throughout the region. They are now widely cultivated in the ideal rich volcanic soil of the area, cementing their place in both Campania's agriculture and its cuisine.

✣ MAKES 1 LOAF

500 g (1 lb 2 oz) strong plain white
  or tipo 0 flour
100 g (3¹/₂ oz) wholemeal plain flour
pinch of salt
25 g (scant 1 oz) fresh yeast
150 ml (5 fl oz) warm milk
100 g (3¹/₂ oz) butter, melted
100 g (3¹/₂ oz) walnuts, freshly
  chopped
50 g (1³/₄ oz) pine nuts

Mix together the two types of flour with a pinch of salt, and make a well in the centre. Dissolve the yeast in the warm milk. Add to the flour with the melted butter. Knead well for 10 minutes until the dough is soft and springy, adding a little warm water if necessary. Add two-thirds of the walnuts and pine nuts, mixing in well. Shape the dough into a ball and put in a large oiled bowl. Cover with a clean tea towel, and leave to rise in a warm place for about 45 minutes.

When the dough has risen, knead once again, then shape into a round loaf and place on a greased and lightly floured baking sheet. Flatten out the dough slightly with your hands and leave to rise for a further 45 minutes. Brush the dough with a little water and sprinkle over the remaining walnuts and pine nuts. Bake in a preheated oven at 240°C (475°F/Gas 9) for about 40 minutes or until the crust is golden. Remove from the oven and serve.

DOLCI
Desserts & pastries

PASTIERA NAPOLETANA
Neapolitan wheat-grain & ricotta Easter tart

Neapolitan cuisine is peppered with dishes that are strongly associated with particular festivals or celebrations, or particular times of the year. *Pastiera napoletana* is one such dish and it is traditionally served at Easter. Although now associated with the Christian calendar, its roots are thought to be much older than this – indeed, centuries old – and lie in the pagan ritual of making offerings to the arrival of spring. Lard is traditionally used for the pastry, which makes it very short and light, but you can use butter or white vegetable shortening, if you prefer.

✣ SERVES 6–8

200 g (7 oz) wheat grain (with the husks removed)
1.5 litres (2^3/$_4$ pints) milk
grated zest of ^{1}/$_2$ lemon
1–2 teaspoons ground cinnamon
1 teaspoon pure vanilla extract
grated zest of ^{1}/$_2$ orange
300 g (10 oz) tipo 00 flour or plain flour
400 g (14 oz) sugar
150 g (5 oz) lard or butter, or half and half of each
4 large eggs, separated, plus 3 extra yolks
300 g (10 oz) ricotta
200 g (7 oz) mixed candied peel, chopped
about 2 tablespoons orange-flower water (available in gourmet food shops and good supermarkets)
salt
icing sugar for dusting

Soak the grain in plenty of cold water for a few days, changing the water every day. Some recipes actually call for the wheat to be soaked for a period of 2 weeks before being used – but just long enough to soften the grain and allow it to expand is enough. (Alternatively you can use ready-to-use precooked wheat, which is available in tins from good Italian delicatessens.) Drain and simmer gently in the milk over a very low heat, covered, for about 4 hours with the grated zest of ^{1}/$_2$ lemon and a pinch of salt. Remove from the heat and drain off any excess liquid, then flavour the grain with the cinnamon, vanilla and the grated zest of ^{1}/$_2$ orange. Leave in the refrigerator overnight to allow the flavour to develop.

Make the shortcrust pastry. Sift the flour and a pinch of salt into a bowl. Add 150 g (5 oz) of the sugar, and rub in the lard or butter with your fingertips until the mixture resembles rough breadcrumbs. Make a well in the centre and add 3 egg yolks. Draw together into a dough, form into a flattish disc, wrap in cling film and leave to rest in the refrigerator for 2 hours.

In the meantime, preheat the oven to 150°C (300°F/Gas 2). Mix the ricotta in a bowl with the remaining 250 g (9 oz) sugar, 4 egg yolks, the candied peel, orange-flower water and 4 beaten egg whites. Roll out the pastry, and use to line a greased round tart tin or pie dish about 30 cm (12 in) in diameter and 7.5 cm (3 in) deep, keeping a little pastry aside for decoration. Add the soaked grain to the ricotta and fold in delicately. Pour into the pastry case. Roll out the remaining pastry into strips (you may need to add a little extra flour here, as the pastry is so short – this will make it easier to work with), and place over the filling in a diamond lattice pattern. Bake in the oven for about 40 minutes or until set and the pastry is golden. Leave to cool, and dust with icing sugar before serving.

CREMA DI CIOCCOLATA
Chocolate cream with citron & orange peel

Carnevale is a celebration that culminates in Mardi Gras ('Fat Tuesday' or Shrove Tuesday). Mardi Gras is seen as one last day of parades and gaiety before Lent. This traditional carnival dessert was formerly made with pig's blood, known as *sanguinaccio*. The Neapolitan version is a rich thick cream usually eaten cold with *savoiardi* biscuits. This is a chocolate-only recipe.

✣ SERVES 4

100 g (3½ oz) plain cocoa powder
450 g (1 lb) caster sugar
4 teaspoons Italian tipo 00 flour
  or plain flour
2 teaspoons cornflour
250 ml (8 fl oz) milk
knob of butter
1 tablespoon pure vanilla extract
1 tablespoon ground cinnamon
50 g (1¾ oz) candied citron and
  orange peel
savoiardi (Italian sponge fingers),
  to serve

In a saucepan, thoroughly mix the cocoa powder, sugar, flour, cornflour, milk, knob of butter, half the vanilla extract and the cinnamon. Cook over a gentle heat until the mixture comes to the boil, stirring all the time. Remove the pan from the heat and add the citron and orange peel and the remaining vanilla. Stir through, then leave to set before serving – the consistency should not be too thick. Serve with *savoiardi* for dipping into the chocolate cream.

Note If you are a real chocoholic, you can add some good-quality grated dark chocolate (at least 70% cocoa solids) to the cream at the same time as the peel, and stir through to melt – this makes the dessert sinfully rich, which seems appropriate given *sanguinaccio*'s association with *Carnevale* and the period preceding Lent.

BISCOTTI AL CIOCCOLATO E MANDORLE
Chocolate & almond biscuits

These biscuits are an old family recipe and a much-loved one. The mixture is rolled out like pastry and cut into any shape you prefer. Almonds grow prolifically in Campania and are an important agricultural crop, turning up in everything from sweets such as sugared almonds (known as *confetti* in Italy) and *torrone* (nougat), to wine and liqueurs.

✣ SERVES 4

300 g (10 oz) Italian tipo 00 flour
  or plain flour
100 g (3½ oz) plain cocoa powder
150 g (5 oz) sugar
1 tablespoon baking powder
1 large egg plus 2 large egg yolks
100 g (3½ oz) almonds, blanched
  and chopped

Preheat the oven to 180°C (350°F/Gas 4). Put the flour in a bowl and make a well in the centre. Add the remaining ingredients, and beat vigorously until smooth (if the mixture is not coming together, you may need to add another egg, but do not make it too wet).

Roll out the mixture to a thickness of ½ cm (¼ in), and cut into shapes using a pastry cutter, or even a glass turned upside down. Arrange on a greased baking sheet, and bake in the oven for 30 minutes until crisp. Cool on a wire rack before eating. These biscuits will keep for up to a week if stored in an airtight container.

BISCOTTI ROCCOCÒ
Almond Christmas biscuits

Roccocò are a speciality of Campania and are typically served as a dessert at Christmas time, but they make an excellent treat at any time of the year. Redolent with spices and citrus, and made in a traditional ring, or doughnut, shape, these crisp biscuits echo the Arab influence on the history and culture of the region, and indeed that of much of Southern Italy.

✛ MAKES ABOUT 20

150 g (5 oz) sweet almonds
300 g (10 oz) Italian tipo 00 flour
300 g (10 oz) sugar
1 tablespoon ammonium bicarbonate
  (see note)
grated zest of 1 lemon
grated zest of 1 orange
good pinch of freshly grated nutmeg
1 teaspoon ground cinnamon
125 ml (4 fl oz) sweet white wine
  or water
125 g (4^1/2 oz) candied citron and
  orange peel, finely chopped
1 large egg, beaten
icing sugar for dusting

Preheat the oven to 180°C (350°F/Gas 4). Blanch the almonds in very hot water for 5 minutes. Peel and arrange in a single layer on a baking sheet. Leave the almonds in the warm oven for a few minutes to dry out, then roughly chop.

On a pastry board, mix the flour with the sugar, almonds, ammonium bicarbonate, lemon and orange zest, nutmeg and cinnamon. Add just enough of the wine or water, a little at a time, to form a stiff dough. Next mix in the citron and orange peel, and form the dough into 20 balls. Shape each ball of dough into a sausage about 15 cm (6 in) long, overlap the ends slightly and join to form flattish rings like doughnuts.

Lightly grease a baking sheet, and arrange the rings in rows. Brush the tops with the beaten egg to glaze, and bake in the oven for about 25 minutes or until golden. Cool a little, dust liberally with icing sugar and serve.

Note The ammonium bicarbonate traditionally used to make these biscuits can be substituted with ^{1}/2 tablespoon baking powder and ^{1}/2 tablespoon bircarbonate of soda.

TORTA CAPRESE
Chocolate almond cake

The island of Capri is a gem, and so is this moist textured cake with chocolate and almonds. The dusting of icing sugar to finish is traditional, and examples of this cake can be found in bakeries and *pasticcerie* throughout Campania. Capri is also famed for its limoncello, and this liqueur gives the cake here its distinctive citrus twist.

✢ SERVES 6–8

250 g (9 oz) butter
6 eggs, separated
250 g (9 oz) sugar
60 ml (2 fl oz) citrus liqueur,
  preferably limoncello
400 g (14 oz) blanched almonds,
  roughly chopped
250 g (9 oz) good-quality dark
  chocolate, roughly chopped
icing sugar for dusting

Preheat the oven to 180°C (350°C/Gas 4). Melt the butter in a bain-marie or in a heatproof bowl over a saucepan of simmering water, then allow to cool slightly. In a large bowl, beat the egg yolks with the sugar and liqueur until creamy. Whip the egg whites and fold into the egg yolk mixture with the butter. Sprinkle in the almonds and chocolate, and fold gently through the mixture. (If the mixture is too runny, add a few more chopped almonds.)

Line a large round cake tin with baking parchment, and pour in the mixture. Bake in the preheated oven for about an hour or until a skewer inserted into the centre of the cake comes out clean. Allow to cool slightly, then dust generously with icing sugar and serve.

Note In this recipe, the almonds and eggs give the cake its body. If you would prefer a smoother texture, simply chop the almonds more finely and grate the chocolate before adding to the mixture. This is how you would usually find it prepared if you bought it from a Campanian bakery.

SFOGLIATELLE RICCE
Semolina & ricotta pastries

Sfogliatelle have a long history that began in the 1700s in the kitchens of the Croce di Lucca monastery, where *sfogliatelle ricce* were prepared for visitors. A later version was made by the cloistered nuns at the Santa Rosa convent on the Amalfi coast. It was in 1818 that *sfogliatelle* were first produced outside the monastery and convent kitchens by Pasquale Pintauro, a baker on Naples' via Toledo, who served them in a seemingly never-ending stream to his customers (the Pintauro bakery still exists today). Soon bakeries and *pasticcerie* all over Naples were imitating him. Today, *sfogliatelle* are considered the queen of Neapolitan pastries. *Sfogliatelle ricce* have a characteristic clam shape and flaky pastry. *Sfogliatelle frolle* are shaped more like an oval bun and are made of a smooth shortcrust pastry. *Sfogliatelle Santa Rosa* have a rich custard cream and black cherry filling; made of the same pastry, they are larger and folded like a turnover.

✣ SERVES 4

For the pastry
350 g (12 oz) Italian tipo 00 flour
  or plain flour
pinch of salt
175 g (6 oz) lard or butter, or half and
  half of each, softened and cut into
  chunks, plus extra, melted, for
  brushing pastry

For the filling
150 g (5 oz) semolina
200 g (7 oz) ricotta
150 g (5 oz) icing sugar
1 tablespoon pure vanilla extract
1 large egg, beaten
85 g (3 oz) candied citron and orange
  peel, finely chopped
pinch of ground cinnamon
icing sugar for dusting

Sift the flour into a large bowl with a pinch of salt. Make a well in the centre. Rub in the butter with your fingertips, then add about 125 ml (4 fl oz) water, and mix to form a dough. Knead for several minutes until smooth. Shape into a ball, wrap in cling film and chill for 2–3 hours.

On a floured work surface, roll out the dough very thinly into a rectangle about 70 x 60 cm (28 x 24 in). Trim the edges. Cut into four equal pieces lengthways, so that you have four strips, each about 70 x 15 cm (28 x 6 in). Brush the melted lard or butter over a strip evenly and generously. Carefully lift the second strip of pastry, and place it over the first. Brush generously and evenly with the lard or butter. Repeat with the remaining strips, so that each one is separated by a layer of shortening. Allow to set. Gently roll up from one short end like a Swiss roll, wrap in cling film and chill for 2–3 hours.

Bring 400 ml (14 fl oz) water to the boil in a saucepan with a pinch of salt. Sprinkle in the semolina and cook for about 5 minutes, stirring all the time with a wooden spoon. Leave to rest in the refrigerator for 2–3 hours.

Preheat the oven to 200°C (400°F/Gas 6). Pass the ricotta through a sieve and add the icing sugar, vanilla, egg, candied peel, cinnamon and cooked semolina. Mix thoroughly and set aside.

Trim the ends of the pastry evenly using a small sharp knife. Cut the roll into 12 discs about 1 cm (1/2 in) thick. Sprinkle lightly with flour, then gently roll out each disc in four directions from the centre so that you have slightly oval shapes. Pick up a pastry oval in the palm of your hand, rolled side down, and cup your hand slightly. Push down gently in the centre of the pastry so that you form a cone. Put some filling in the pocket, then lightly squeeze to form a clam shape. Press down tightly to seal the edges; pinch the narrow end slightly to accentuate the clam shape. Repeat with the remaining pastry. Brush with extra melted lard or butter. Bake in the oven on a greased baking sheet for 20–25 minutes until golden, brushing with melted lard or butter once or twice as they cook. Serve warm, dusted with icing sugar.

ZEPPOLE DI SAN GIUSEPPE
Deep-fried pastry puffs

Traditionally made to celebrate the Feast of Saint Joseph on 19 March, which is observed throughout Italy, these pastries, or at least the consuming of them, are a time-honoured ritual in Naples. Eating *zeppole* on St Joseph's Day is as ingrained a custom as the traditional wearing of red clothing and the outdoor market on via Guglielmo Sanfelice and via Medina selling caged birds and toys to excited children. *Pasticcerie* and *friggitorie* (shops selling fried food) all over the city serve them by the dozen, piping hot, to the queues of hungry customers.

✣ SERVES 4

250 g (9 oz) butter
pinch of salt
400 g (14 oz) Italian tipo 00 flour
  or plain flour
12 large egg yolks
3 large egg whites
vegetable oil for deep-frying
icing sugar for dusting
500 ml (16 fl oz) milk
200 g (7 oz) sugar
1 tablespoon pure vanilla extract
250 g (9 oz) black cherry jam,
  to decorate

Put 500 ml (16 fl oz) water, the butter and a pinch of salt into a pan and bring to the boil. Remove from the heat and sprinkle in the flour, stirring continuously until the mixture comes away from the sides of the pan. Allow to cool a little, then beat in 9 of the egg yolks and the 3 egg whites using a wooden spoon. Transfer the mixture to a pastry bag and, using a large piping nozzle, pipe small ring-shaped doughnuts onto greaseproof paper or similar.

Heat enough oil for deep-frying in a heavy deep-sided saucepan over a medium-high heat. To test whether the oil is hot enough, carefully slide one of the pastries into the pan using a metal spatula or egg slice – it should sizzle straight away. Cooking in batches, deep-fry the pastries for 5 minutes until golden. Remove from the oil using a slotted spoon, and drain on kitchen paper. Cool slightly, then dust liberally with icing sugar.

Meanwhile, to make the *crema pasticciera* (custard cream), combine the milk, sugar, the remaining 3 egg yolks and the vanilla in a small saucepan. Bring to the boil over a gentle heat, stirring until thickened. Use to decorate the *zeppole*, piping a little custard cream into the centre of each one. Dot a teaspoonful of black cherry jam on top of the custard cream, and serve the *zeppole* warm or cold.

FRITTELLE
Sweet potato fritters

A *cucina povera* recipe, these crisp, sweet fritters are typical of the *passatèmpi* or *merende* (snacks) sold on the street stalls and kiosks all around Naples. They are at their best and most irresistible when served freshly made and piping hot – *frienn' magnann'*.

✛ SERVES 4

400 g (14 oz) floury potatoes
450 g (1 lb) Italian tipo 00 flour
  or plain flour
25 g (3/4 oz) fresh yeast
a little milk
1 tablespoon sugar
100 ml (3¹/2 fl oz) vegetable oil plus
  extra for deep-frying
2 large eggs
grated zest of 1 lemon
caster sugar for sprinkling

Boil, peel and mash the potatoes. Make a well in the flour and add the yeast, a little milk and all the other ingredients. Knead vigorously for 15 minutes. Break off into about 40 equal-sized balls, each the size of a tablespoon. Roll out into sausage-like strips and join the ends together, overlapping them slightly and pinching gently together to form rings. Lay out on a greased baking sheet, cover with a clean tea towel or cloth, and leave to rise for about 2 hours in a warm, draught-free place.

Heat enough oil for deep-frying in a large deep-sided heavy saucepan over a medium to medium-high heat. To test whether the oil is hot enough, carefully drop in one of the *frittelle* – it should sizzle straight away. Deep-fry the *frittelle* in batches for 5 minutes until golden brown. Remove from the oil using a slotted spoon, and drain on kitchen paper. Sprinkle with caster sugar, and serve immediately.

GNOCCHETTI FRITTI ALLA ANNARELLA
Sweet gnocchetti fritters

Made in the same way as fresh savoury potato gnocchi, this dessert recipe is a family one. Again, as with the *frittelle*, these sweet morsels are at their best when served straight from pan to table.

✛ SERVES 4

500 g (1 lb 2 oz) Italian tipo 00 flour
  or plain flour
pinch of salt
5 large eggs, beaten
150 g (5 oz) sugar
1 tablespoon pure vanilla extract
1 tablespoon baking powder
vegetable oil for deep-frying
icing sugar for dusting

Put the flour in a bowl and make a well in the centre. Add the salt, eggs, sugar and vanilla extract. Mix well until smooth. Add the baking powder and continue mixing for about 10 minutes until the dough is smooth and elastic. Leave the dough to rest in the refrigerator for 1 hour.

To make the *gnocchetti*, knead the dough gently for a couple of minutes, then quickly roll out into finger-thick sausage-like strips. Cut up into 60 or so small pieces about 2.5 cm (1 in) long, or the size of ordinary gnocchi.

Heat enough oil for deep-frying in a heavy saucepan over a medium to medium-high heat. Add the *gnocchetti* a few at time, deep-frying for about 5 minutes until golden. Remove from the pan using a slotted spoon, and drain on kitchen paper. Continue frying in batches until all the dough has been used. Dust with icing sugar and serve piping hot.

BABÀ
Yeast cake soaked in rum syrup

The babà arrived in Naples with the Bourbon court of the eighteenth century, the cooks in the royal household bringing the recipe with them from France. In their inimitable style, though, Neapolitans have made babà their own, and it is available from pastry shops all over the city both in the traditional large ring (kughelhopf) shape and baked in individual baba moulds that look a little like flower pots. Babà are always well soaked in syrup, usually rum-based, although limoncello versions are becoming popular. Babà should be eaten on the same day it is made, or the next day at the latest.

⊹ SERVES 6–8

25 g (scant 1 oz) fresh yeast
350 g (12 oz) tipo 00 flour
  or plain flour
pinch of salt
250 g (9 oz) butter
5 large eggs, beaten
1¹/₂ tablespoons sugar
60 ml (2 fl oz) single cream

For the syrup
100 g (3¹/₂ oz) sugar
200 ml (7 fl oz) rum or limoncello

For the glacé icing (optional)
120 g (4 oz) icing sugar
3–4 tablespoons rum or limoncello

Mix the yeast with a little warm water. Add a few tablespoons of the flour and mix to a smooth paste. Leave to rise for about an hour in a warm place.

When the mixture has doubled in size, combine with the remaining flour, salt, butter and eggs. Mix vigorously to a dough, kneading with your hands until it comes away from the sides of the bowl. Add the sugar and cream. Continue kneading for a few minutes, then transfer to a high-sided buttered babà mould. The dough should not come up past a third of the mould's height. Leave to rise again for about 2 hours in a dry, draught-free place. Bake in a preheated oven at 200°C (400°F/Gas 6) for 20 minutes until golden.

In the meantime, make a syrup by bringing 400 ml (14 fl oz) water to the boil with the sugar and rum or limoncello. Remove the babà from the oven and pour over the syrup, allowing it to soak into the cake. Allow to cool.

If you like, you can drizzle a thin glacé icing over the top, letting it run down the sides but not cover the babà completely. To make the icing, put the icing sugar in a bowl, and mix in the rum (if you used the rum syrup) or limoncello (if you used limoncello) a tablespoon at a time until the icing is smooth and runny. Remember that the icing will set slightly once on the cake, but you do not want it to be so runny that it slides off completely. Drizzle the icing around the top of the cake so that it runs down the sides in 'rivulets' and leave it to set before serving.

FESTIVALS & CELEBRATIONS

While it is true that the emphasis in the cuisine of Naples and surrounding Campania is not on desserts, there is definitely a love of sweet things that is perhaps not so prevalent in other parts of Italy. You can start and end your day with something sweet, whether it is bought from a bakery or *pasticceria*, or made at home. There are numerous sweet pastries to choose from, and special cakes and tarts associated with particular places, such as the *torta caprese*. Fruit appears in various forms, and dessert will often simply be a serving of fresh fruit such as citrus fruits, figs, peaches, apricots or cherries. Use is also made of the region's abundance of nuts, such as almonds, chestnuts and walnuts, in *torrone* (nougat) and other sweets such as *confetti* (sugared almonds), as well as biscuits, pastries and cakes. And then, of course, there are the ice creams: *gelati*, *semifreddi*, *sorbetti*, *spumoni*, *ghiacciate* (syrup-flavoured shaved ice) and *granite*. Ice cream and ices are a delight on a hot summer's day, and range from simple *gelati* flavoured with the region's outstanding citrus fruits or pistachios, to the more elaborate *spumoni*, rich with nuts.

Many of Campania's most distinctive and well known desserts and pastries, like some of the best-loved savoury dishes, are traditionally linked with festivals and celebrations, or particular times of the year. *Carnevale*, Lent, Easter, Christmas, saints' days – where there is a celebration or special occasion, there is usually a pastry or dessert specially served to mark the event. A special chocolate cream, *sanguinaccio* (page 140), is eaten during carnival, for instance.

Pastiera napoletana (see pages 138–9) is eaten at Easter and has been for centuries; however, much further in the past this ricotta and wheat-grain cake was part of ceremonial offerings to spring, and in particular to the siren Parthenope. Parthenope has long been associated with Naples in legend; it is said that following her failure to lure Odysseus onto the rocks of the Li Galli Islands off the Amalfi coast, she threw herself into the sea in despair and was washed up on the shore of the Bay of Naples from which the settlement of Naples eventually grew. The rich *pastiera napoletana* is usually served in thin slices for breakfast, over the Easter week.

Zeppole di San Giuseppe appear every year for the Feast of Saint Joseph on 19 March in their *bignè* (choux pastry) form, topped with custard cream and cherry jam. The other type of *zeppole*, made of a simpler dough, is usually served at Christmas. So, too, are the traditional spice biscuits *mostaccioli* and *roccocò* (see page 141).

Perhaps the most exuberant of all Neapolitan desserts are *struffoli* (see pages 154–5). Made to signify abundance and eaten at Christmas, these fritters are soaked in honey syrup and decorated freely with hundreds and thousands, candied citron and orange peel.

STRUFFOLI
Christmas fritters with honey & candied peel

These typical Christmas fritters symbolize abundance for Neapolitans. In a society which grew from roots where for most people food was scarce and making a living from the land was difficult, *struffoli* are a considered a symbol of good luck, as well as a food of celebration. Anyone who eats *struffoli* is supposed to enjoy a prosperous and plentiful year ahead.

✛ SERVES 4

400 g (14 oz) Italian tipo 00 flour
  or plain flour
30 g (1 oz) butter, roughly cubed
3 large eggs plus 3 yolks
1 tablespoon brandy
250 g (9 oz) sugar
pinch of salt
grated zest of 1 lemon
grated zest of 1 orange
250 g (9 oz) honey
150 g (5 oz) orange and citron
  peel, finely chopped, plus extra,
  to decorate
hundreds and thousands, to decorate
silver and gold dragees, to decorate
angelica and glacé cherries, halved,
  to decorate
vegetable oil for deep-frying

On a pastry board or in a large bowl, use a metal spatula to combine the flour with the butter, eggs, brandy, 1 tablespoon of the sugar, a pinch of salt and the grated lemon and orange zest. Mix well and leave to rest in the refrigerator for about an hour. Roll out the pastry into very thin strips and cut into small pieces.

Heat the oil in a high-sided heavy saucepan over a medium heat. To test whether the oil is hot enough for frying, fry a small piece of the *struffoli* dough first – it should sizzle straight away. Deep-fry the *struffoli* for 5 minutes, a few at a time, until golden. Remove with a slotted spoon and drain on kitchen paper.

Put the honey and remaining sugar in a very large saucepan with 60 ml (2 fl oz) water. Bring to the boil and continue boiling until the foam that forms on the top has disappeared completely and the honey has turned a light amber colour. Add the *struffoli* and finely chopped candied peel. Stir over a very gentle heat until they are all coated with the honey glaze.

Use a wooden spoon to turn out the *struffoli* onto a serving plate, and arrange into a pyramid, ring or any shape you fancy. Sprinkle with the hundreds and thousands, and decorate with the extra peel, silver and gold dragees, and small pieces of angelica and glacé cherries. To eat, simply break off individual *struffoli* with your fingers, and enjoy with a cup of fine-quality Neapolitan coffee.

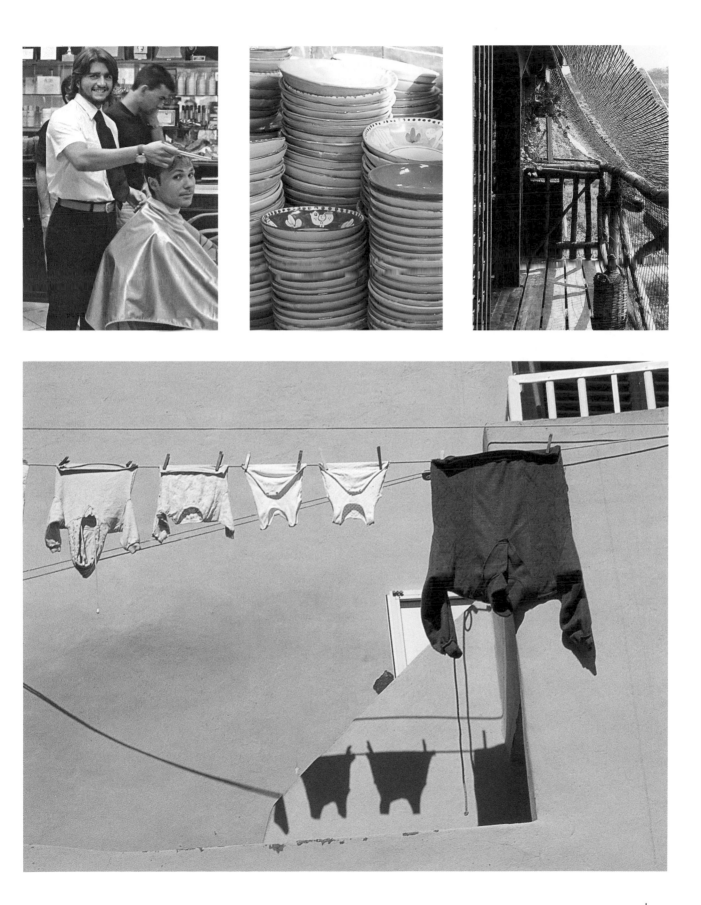

INDEX

alici ripiene, 89
almonds: almond Christmas biscuits, 131
    chocolate and almond biscuits, 140
    chocolate almond cake, 144
anchovies: boned and stuffed, 89
    pizza with capers, olives and, 132
artichokes: baked artichokes stuffed with mozzarella, 19
    braised potatoes and, 114
    deep-fried artichokes, 120
    potato and artichoke soup, 28
aubergines: baked with tomatoes and mozzarella, 116
    fried aubergine and provolone sandwiches, 115
    maccheroncelli with cherry tomatoes and, 54
    roasted peppers stuffed with olives, capers and, 123
    spicy ratatouille of peppers, potatoes and, 120

babà, 151
baccalà alla Francese, 100
baccalà alla Napoletana, 100
baccalà in pastella, 87
beans: bread soup with cannellini beans and escarole, 26
    cannellini bean soup, 23
    pasta with cannellini beans, 54
    stewed beans in cherry tomato sauce, 109
    white bean and escarole soup, 23
    white bean salad with tuna, spring onions and olives, 113
beef: beef, onion and wine sauce, 35
    beef stew with peas and rosemary, 71
    classic slow-cooked meat and tomato sauce, 55
    meatballs in tomato sauce, 84
    meatloaf with courgette and mashed potato, 70
    rocket salad with warm grilled beef, cherry tomatoes and basil, 87
    slices of beef with tomato and oregano, 70
biscotti al cioccolato e mandorle, 140
biscotti roccocò, 131
biscuits 131, 140
bocconcini del prete, 103

braciolone alla Napoletana, 74
bread: basic dough, 133
    bread soup, 26
    mozzarella in a carriage, 17
    olive bread, 135
    rosemary bread, 133
    walnut bread, 135
broad beans: stewed broad beans, 28
    tubetti with fresh broad beans, 56
bucatini alla 'settembrini', 49
bucatini con i peperoncini, 34
bucatini with green peperoncini, tomatoes and basil, 34

cakes, 144, 151
calamari e gamberoni al profumo di mare, 16
calzone di ricotta e salame, 130
cannellini beans *see* beans
capretto uova e formaggio, 71
carciofi con mozzarella, 19
carciofi e patate, 114
carciofi indorati e fritti, 120
cefalo alla marinara, 93
cefalo arrosto, 93
cheese, 8–9
    baked artichokes stuffed with mozzarella, 19
    baked aubergine with tomatoes and mozzarella, 116
    baked courgettes and mozzarella, 121
    baked mini omelettes with provolone, ham and tomato, 103
    baked pennette with four cheeses, 52
    braised kid with eggs and, 71
    fresh pasta bake with ricotta, 52
    fried aubergine and provolone sandwiches, 115
    fusilli with ricotta, tomatoes and Parmesan, 34
    mozzarella and provolone fritters, 103
    mozzarella di bufala, 45
    mozzarella in a carriage, 17
    Neapolitan wheat-grain and ricotta Easter tart, 138
    ricotta and salami calzone, 130
    semolina and ricotta pastries, 146
    tomato, basil and mozzarella salad, 113

chicken roulades in tomato sauce, 68
chickpeas, pasta and, 40
chillies: bucatini with green peperoncini, tomatoes and basil, 34
chocolate: chocolate and almond biscuits, 140
    chocolate almond cake, 144
    chocolate cream with citron and orange peel, 140
Christmas biscuits, 131
Christmas fritters, 154
clams: clams sautéed in garlic and oil, 92
    linguine with tomatoes and, 47
    spaghetti with prawns, squid and, 42
coffee, 110
conchiglie con olio e limone, 62
conchiglie with oil and lemon, 62
coniglio alla Nonna Rita, 78
coniglio all'Ischitana, 78
courgettes: baby zucchini and potato stew, 114
    baked courgettes and mozzarella, 121
    meatloaf with mashed potato and, 70
    pasta with spring vegetables, 37
    tricolour pasta, 49
    with eggs, pancetta and Parmesan, 115
cozze al pepe, 14
crema di cioccolata, 140

Easter tart, 138
eggs: baked mini omelettes, 103
    braised kid with cheese and, 71
    potato frittata, 104
escarole: bread soup with cannellini beans and, 26
    white bean and escarole soup, 23

fagioli in umido, 109
fagiolini indorati e fritti, 109
farfalle con tonno e piselli, 46
farfalle with tuna and peas, 46
fettine alla pizzaiola, 70
le fettine di pulcinella, 83
fish, 90–1
frittata di patate, 104
frittelle, 149
fritters, 103, 149, 153, 154
fritto di mozzarella e provola, 103
frittura di calamari e scampi, 92
fruit, 11, 153

fusilli con la ricotta, 34
fusilli with ricotta, tomatoes and Parmesan, 34
gnocchetti e cozze in brodetto, 22
gnocchetti fritti alla annarella, 149
green beans, fried, 109
grey mullet: grilled marinated grey mullet, 93
    with spring onion and parsley, 93
honey, Christmas fritters with, 154

impasto per pane, 133
insalata Caprese, 113
insalata di carne, 87
insalata di fagioli, 113
insalata di riso, 63

kid braised with eggs and cheese, 71

lasagnette con la ricotta, 52
lentils: country-style sausages with, 77
    pasta and lentils, 40
linguine con funghi e gamberoni, 58
linguine con la pancetta, 49
linguine con vongole e pomodori, 47
linguine: with clams and tomatoes, 47
    with mushrooms and king prawns, 58
    with pancetta and tomato sauce, 49

maccheroncelli: with aubergine and cherry tomatoes, 54
    with tomato and chilli, 32
maccheroncelli arrabbiati, 32
maccheroncelli con le melanzane, 54
meatballs in tomato sauce, 84
meatloaf with courgette and mashed potato, 70
melanzane in carrozza, 115
minestra di scarole e fagioli, 23
mozzarella in carrozza, 17
mozzarella di bufala, 45
mushrooms: linguine with king prawns and, 58
    veal in white wine with cherry tomatoes and, 83
mussels: gnocchetti sardi and mussel soup, 22
    peppered mussels, 14

Neapolitan wheat-grain and ricotta Easter tart, 138

octopus sauce, vermicelli with, 46
olive bread, 135
olive oil, 21
omelettes, baked mini, 103

pancetta, linguine with tomato sauce and, 49
pane al rosmarino, 133
pane di noce, 135
pane di olive, 135
Parmigiana di melanzane, 116
pasta, 10–11, 30–62
pasta and chickpeas, 40
pasta and lentils, 40
pasta con salsiccia piccante e patate, 130
pasta e ceci, 40
pasta e fagioli, 54
pasta e lenticchie, 40
pasta e zucca, 62
pasta per pizze, 129
pasta with cannellini beans, 54
pasta with pumpkin, 62
pasta with spring vegetables, 37
pastiera Napoletana, 138
pastries, 153
    deep-fried puffs, 148
    semolina and ricotta, 146
peas: beef stew with rosemary and, 71
    braised kid with eggs and cheese, 71
    farfalle with tuna and, 46
pennette al formaggio al forno, 52
pennette primavera, 37
peperoni imbottite, 123
peppers: roasted peppers stuffed with aubergine, olives and capers, 123
    spicy ratatouille of aubergines, potatoes and, 120
petto di pollo aromatico, 68
pizza, 124–32
    basic dough, 129
    pizza Margherita, 129
    pizza marinara, 129
    spicy sausage and potato pizza, 130
    with capers, olives and anchovies, 132
pizza capperi, olive e acciughe, 132
polpette alla Napoletana, 84
pork roulade with prosciutto, Parmesan and parsley, 74
potatoes: baby zucchini and potato stew, 114

braised artichokes and, 114
    meatloaf with courgette and mashed potato, 70
    pan-fried sausages with new potatoes and chilli, 76
    potato and artichoke soup, 28
    potato frittata, 104
    spicy ratatouille of peppers, aubergines and, 120
    sweet potato fritters, 149
prawns: linguine with mushrooms and king prawns, 58
    pan-fried squid and king prawns, 16
    spaghetti with squid, clams and, 42
    squid stuffed with shellfish and bread, 96
pumpkin, pasta with, 62

rabbit: braised with onions and brandy, 78
    braised with wine, tomato and herbs, 78
ragù di carne, 55
ratatouille, spicy, 120
red mullet, grilled marinated, 94
rice: creamy rice with fresh tomato and basil sauce, 64
    rice salad with tuna, eggs and fontina, 63
riso bella Napoli, 64
rocket salad with warm grilled beef, 87
rosemary bread, 133

salads: rice with tuna, eggs and fontina, 63
    rocket with warm grilled beef, 87
    tomato, basil and mozzarella, 113
    white bean salad with tuna, 113
salsa genovese, 35
salsicce al cartocchio, 76
salsicce alla contadina, 77
salsicce del prete, 76
salt cod: battered salt cod fillets, 87
    with tomato, olives and capers, 100
    with onion and wine, 100
sausages: charcoal-grilled sausages in a parcel, 76
    country-style sausages with lentils, 77
    pan-fried sausages with new potatoes and chilli, 76

spicy sausage and potato pizza, 130
scaloppine di montagna, 83
scampi, fried squid and, 92
sea bass with oil and lemon, 94
seafood, 90–1
semolina and ricotta pastries, 146
seppie imbottite, 96
sfogliatelle ricce, 146
Sorrento cheeses, 8–9
soups, 22–9
soutè di vongole, 92
spaghetti: with prawns, squid and clams, 42
    with tomatoes and basil, 37
    with tuna, anchovies, tomatoes and olives, 41
spaghetti al filetto di pomodoro, 37
spaghetti alla caprese, 41
spaghetti alla rosinella, 42
spezzatino con i piselli, 71
spigola al forno, 94
squid: fried scampi and, 92
    pan-fried king prawns and, 16
    spaghetti with prawns, clams and, 42
    squid stuffed with shellfish and bread, 96
struffoli, 153, 154
stufato di verdure, 120
sweet gnocchetti fritters, 149
sweet potato fritters, 149

tart, wheat-grain and ricotta, 138
tomatoes, 9–10
    baked aubergine with mozzarella and, 116
    braised rabbit with wine, herbs and, 78
    bucatini with green peperoncini, basil and, 34
    classic slow-cooked meat and tomato sauce, 55
    creamy rice with fresh tomato and basil sauce, 64
    fusilli with ricotta, Parmesan and, 34
    linguine with clams and, 47
    linguine with pancetta and tomato sauce, 49
    maccheroncelli with aubergine and cherry tomatoes, 54
    maccheroncelli with chilli and, 32
    meatballs in tomato sauce, 84

salt cod fillets with olives, capers and, 100
spaghetti with basil and, 37
spaghetti with tuna, anchovies, olives and, 41
stewed beans in cherry tomato sauce, 109
tomato, basil and mozzarella salad, 113
tricolour pasta, 49
veal in white wine with cherry tomatoes and mushrooms, 83
torta Caprese, 144
tortino Napoletana, 70
tricolour pasta, 49
triglie del pescatore, 94
tubetti con le fave, 56
tubetti with fresh broad beans, 56
tuna: farfalle with peas and, 46
    rice salad with eggs, fontina and, 63
    spaghetti with anchovies, tomatoes, olives and, 41
    white bean salad with spring onions, olives and, 113

veal: veal scaloppine with prosciutto, capers and mushrooms, 83
    veal in white wine with cherry tomatoes and mushrooms, 83
vermicelli aglio e olio, 63
vermicelli con sugo di polipi, 46
vermicelli: with garlic and oil, 63
    with octopus sauce, 46

walnut bread, 135
wheat-grain and ricotta Easter tart, 138
white bean and escarole soup, 23
wines, 7–8, 72

yeast cake soaked in rum syrup, 151

zeppole di San Giuseppe, 148
zucchette e patate, 114
zucchine uova e formaggio, 115
zucchini con la mozzarella, 121
zuppa di fagioli, 23
zuppa di fagioli e scarola, 26
zuppa di fave secche, 28
zuppa di patate e carciofi, 28

With many thanks to Manuela Barzan, Director of I.R.V.A.T. (Istituto per la Valorizzazione e la Tutela dei Prodotti Regionali), an association of provincial councils and chambers of commerce in Campania for the promotion of regional products on a global level.

PUBLISHING DIRECTOR: Rosemary Wilkinson
PROJECT EDITOR: Siobhán O'Connor
TRANSLATION: I.R.V.A.T.
DESIGNER: Sue Rose, Casebourne Rose Design Associates
RECIPE PHOTOGRAPHS: Frank Wieder
HOME ECONOMIST: Kate Moseley; ADDITIONAL PHOTO SHOOT: Wendy Sweetser
NAPLES PHOTOGRAPHY: Hannah Mornement
COVER DESIGNER: Lucy Parissi
COVER PHOTOGRAPH: Hannah Mornement

Printed and bound by Tien Wah Press, Singapore